# CHANGES
## Anthology

**SERIES EDITORS**
Margaret Iveson
Samuel Robinson

**EDITORIAL CONSULTANT**
Alan Simpson

**LITERATURE CONSULTANT**
Rivka Cranley

**TEACHER CONSULTANTS**
Bill Talbot
Karen Brust
Janet Hancock
Wendy Mathieu
Kathy Smith

PRENTICE HALL CANADA INC.

ISBN 0-13-017096-8

Anthologist: Todd Mercer
Researchers: Monika Croydon, Catherine Rondina

A Ligature, Inc. Book
Cover Illustration: Laura Phillips

**Canadian Cataloguing in Publication Data**

Main entry under title:

Changes : anthology

(MultiSource)
ISBN 0-13-017096-8

1. Change—Literary collections.   2. Children's
literature.   I. Iveson, Margaret L., 1948–
II. Robinson, Sam, 1937–     .   III. Series.
PZ5.C55 1993      j808.8'0355      C92–094877–4

Printed and bound in Canada

  4 5 6 7 DWF 98 97

The universe is change;
our life is what our thoughts make it.

MARCUS AURELIUS ANTONINUS
(A.D. 121–180)

# Contents

# He Was So Little

He was so little he had to sit on a book
To be tall enough to reach his spoon and fork.
Yet, when his mother began to put on his bib,
He pushed it away. "I'm not a baby," he snapped.
And he sat very straight and tried to look adult.

"How are you getting along?" my father asked.
"Would you like me to spread your bread?"
"No, thank you," he replied. "I prefer it bare."

It wasn't really funny, not funny at all.
He looked bewildered and wounded when they all laughed.

I wanted to make them stop, to scream at them,
"Can't you remember what it was like to be small?
Didn't you ever, ever make a mistake?"
I wanted to shout, but I did not speak one word.

And, as their laughter died and his hot cheeks cooled,
I looked at myself and caught the smile on my face.
It's queer sometimes, being this age I am.
It's like being out on a battlefield in a war
—But never being quite sure whose side you're on.

JEAN LITTLE

# Raymond's Run

Toni Cade Bambara

I don't have much work to do around the house like some girls. My mother does that. And I don't have to earn my pocket money by hustling; George runs errands for the big boys and sells Christmas cards. And anything else that's got to get done, my father does. All I have to do in life is mind my brother Raymond, which is enough.

Sometimes I slip and say my little brother Raymond. But as any fool can see he's much bigger and he's older too. But a lot of people call him my little brother cause he needs looking after cause he's not quite right. And a lot of smart mouths got lots to say about that too, especially when George was minding him. But now, if anybody has anything to say to Raymond, anything to say about his big head, they have to come by me. And I don't play the dozens or believe in standing around with somebody in my face doing a lot of talking. I much rather just knock you down and take my chances even if I am a little girl with skinny arms and a squeaky voice, which is how I got the name Squeaky. And if things get too rough, I run. And as anybody can tell you, I'm the fastest thing on two feet.

There is no track meet that I don't win the first place medal. I used to win the twenty-yard dash when I was a little kid in kindergarten. Nowadays, it's the fifty-yard dash. And tomorrow I'm subject to run the quarter-mile relay all by myself and come in first, second, and third. The big kids call me Mercury cause I'm the swiftest thing in the neighborhood. Everybody knows that—except two people who know better, my father and me. He can beat me to Amsterdam Avenue with me having a two fire-hydrant headstart and him running with his hands in his pockets and whistling. But that's private information. Cause can you imagine some thirty-five-year-old man stuffing himself into PAL shorts to race little kids? So as far as everyone's concerned, I'm the fastest and that goes for Gretchen, too, who has put out the tale that she is going to win the first-place medal this year. Ridiculous. In the second place, she's got short legs. In the third place, she's got freckles. In the first place, no one can beat me and that's all there is to it.

I'm standing on the corner admiring the weather and about to take a stroll down Broadway so I can practice my breathing exercises, and I've got Raymond walking on the inside close to the buildings, cause he's subject to fits of fantasy and starts thinking he's a circus performer and that the curb is a tightrope strung high in the air. And sometimes after a rain he likes to step down off his tightrope right into the gutter and slosh around getting his shoes and cuffs wet. Then I get it when I get home. Or sometimes if you don't watch him he'll dash across traffic to the island in the middle of Broadway and give the pigeons a fit. Then I have to go behind him apologizing to all the old people sitting around trying to get some sun and getting all upset with the pigeons fluttering around them, scattering their newspapers and upsetting the waxpaper lunches in their laps. So I keep Raymond on the inside of me, and he plays like he's driving a stage coach which is O.K. by me so long as he doesn't run me over or interrupt my breathing exercises, which I have to do on account of I'm serious about my running, and I don't care who knows it.

Now some people like to act like things come easy to them, won't let on that they practice. Not me. I'll high-prance down 34th Street like a rodeo pony to keep my knees strong even if it does get my mother uptight so that she walks ahead like she's not with me, don't know me, is all by herself on a shopping trip, and I am somebody else's crazy child. Now you take Cynthia Procter for instance. She's just the opposite. If there's a test tomorrow, she'll say something like, "Oh, I guess I'll play hand-ball this afternoon and watch television tonight," just to let you know she ain't thinking about the test. Or like last week when she won the spelling bee for the millionth time, "A good thing you got 'receive,' Squeaky, cause I would have got it wrong. I completely forgot about the spelling bee." And she'll clutch the lace on her blouse like it was a narrow escape. Oh, brother. But of course when I pass her house on my early morning trots around the block, she is practicing the scales on the piano over and over and over and over. Then in music class she always lets herself get bumped around so she falls accidently on purpose onto the piano stool and is so surprised to find herself sitting there that she decides just for fun to try out the ole keys. And what do you know—Chopin's waltzes just spring out of her fingertips and she's the most surprised thing in the world. A regular prodigy. I could kill people like that. I stay up all night studying the words for the spelling bee. And you can see me any time of day practicing running. I never walk if I can trot, and shame on Raymond if he can't keep up. But of course he does, cause if he hangs back someone's liable to walk up to him and get smart, or take his allowance from him, or ask him where he got that great big pumpkin head. People are so stupid sometimes.

So I'm strolling down Broadway breathing out and breathing in on counts of seven, which is my lucky number, and here comes Gretchen and her sidekicks: Mary Louise, who used to be a friend of mine when she first moved to Harlem from Baltimore and got beat up by everybody till I took up for her on account of her mother and my mother used to sing in the same choir when they were young girls, but people ain't grateful, so now she hangs out with the new girl Gretchen and talks about me like a dog; and Rosie, who is as fat as I am skinny and has a big mouth where Raymond is concerned and is too stupid to know that there is not a big deal of difference between herself and Raymond and that she can't afford to throw stones. So they are steady coming up Broadway and I see right away that it's going to be one of those Dodge City scenes cause the street ain't that big and they're close to the buildings just as we are. First I think I'll step into the candy store and look over the new comics and let them pass. But that's chicken and I've got a reputation to consider. So then I think I'll just walk straight on through them or even over them if necessary. But as they get to me, they slow down. I'm ready to fight, cause like I said I don't feature a whole lot of chit-chat, I much prefer to just knock you down right from the jump and save everybody a lotta precious time.

"You signing up for the May Day races?" smiles

Mary Louise, only it's not a smile at all. A dumb question like that doesn't deserve an answer. Besides, there's just me and Gretchen standing there really, so no use wasting my breath talking to shadows.

"I don't think you're going to win this time," says Rosie, trying to signify with her hands on her hips all salty, completely forgetting that I have whupped her behind many times for less salt than that.

"I always win cause I'm the best," I say straight at Gretchen who is, as far as I'm concerned, the only one talking in the ventriloquist-dummy routine. Gretchen smiles, but it's not a smile, and I'm thinking that girls never really smile at each other because they don't know how and don't want to know how and there's probably no one to teach us how, cause grown-up girls don't know either. Then they all look at Raymond who has just brought his mule team to a standstill. And they're about to see what trouble they can get into through him.

"What grade you in now, Raymond?"

"You got anything to say to my brother, you say it to me, Mary Louise Williams of Raggedy Town, Baltimore."

"What are you, his mother?" sasses Rosie.

"That's right, Fatso. And the next word out of any-body and I'll be *their* mother too." So they just stand there and Gretchen shifts from one leg to the other and so do they. Then Gretchen puts her hands on her hips and is about to say something with her freckle-face self but doesn't. Then she walks around me looking me up and down but keeps walking up Broadway, and her sidekicks follow her. So me and Raymond smile at each other and he says, "Gidyap" to his team and I continue with my breathing exercises, strolling down Broadway toward the ice man on 145th with not a care in the world cause I am Miss Quicksilver herself.

I take my time getting to the park on May Day because the track meet is the last thing on the program. The biggest thing on the program is the May Pole dancing, which I can do without, thank you, even if my mother thinks it's a shame I don't take part and act like a girl for a change. You'd think my mother'd be grateful not to have to make me a white organdy dress with a big satin sash and buy me new white baby-doll shoes that can't be taken out of the box till the big day. You'd think she'd be glad her daughter ain't out there prancing around a May Pole getting the new clothes all dirty and sweaty and trying to act like a fairy or a flower or whatever you're supposed to be when you should be trying to be yourself, whatever that is, which is, as far as I am concerned, a poor Black girl who really can't afford to buy shoes and a new dress you wear only once a lifetime cause it won't fit next year.

I was once a strawberry in a Hansel and Gretel pageant when I was in nursery school and didn't have no better sense than to dance on tiptoe with my arms in a circle over my head doing umbrella steps and being a perfect fool just so my mother and father could come dressed up and clap. You'd think they'd know better than to encourage that kind of nonsense. I am not a strawberry. I do not dance on my toes. I run. That is what I am all about. So I always come late to the May Day program, just in time to get my number pinned on and lay in the grass till they announce the fifty-yard dash.

I put Raymond in the little swings, which is a tight squeeze this year and will be impossible next year. Then I look around for Mr. Pearson, who pins the numbers on. I'm really looking for Gretchen if you want to know the truth, but she's not around. The park is jam-packed. Parents in hats and corsages and breast-pocket handkerchiefs peeking up. Kids in white dresses and light-blue suits. The parkees unfolding chairs and chasing the rowdy kids from Lenox as if they had no right to be there. The big guys with their caps on backwards, leaning against the fence swirling the basketballs on the tips of their fingers, waiting for all these crazy people to clear out the park so they can play. Most of the kids in my class are carrying bass drums and glockenspiels and flutes. You'd think they'd put in a few bongos or something for real like that.

Then here comes Mr. Pearson with his clipboard and his cards and pencils and whistles and safety pins and fifty million other things he's always dropping all over the place with his clumsy self. He sticks out in a crowd because he's on stilts. We used to call him Jack and the Beanstalk to get him mad. But I'm the only one that can outrun him and get away, and I'm too grown for that silliness now.

"Well, Squeaky," he says, checking my name off the list and handing me number seven and two pins. And I'm thinking he's got no right to call me Squeaky, if I can't call him Beanstalk.

"Hazel Elizabeth Deborah Parker," I correct him and tell him to write it down on his board.

"Well, Hazel Elizabeth Deborah Parker, going to give someone else a break this year?" I squint at him real hard to see if he is seriously thinking I should lose the race on purpose just to give someone else a break. "Only six girls running this time," he continues, shaking his head sadly like it's my fault all of New York didn't turn out in sneakers. "That new girl should give you a run for your money." He looks around the park for Gretchen like a periscope in a submarine movie. "Wouldn't it be a nice gesture if you were . . . to ahhh . . ."

I give him such a look he couldn't finish putting that

idea into words. Grownups got a lot of nerve sometimes. I pin number seven to myself and stomp away, I'm so burnt. And I go straight for the track and stretch out on the grass while the band winds up with, "Oh, the Monkey Wrapped His Tail Around the Flag Pole," which my teacher calls by some other name. The man on the loudspeaker is calling everyone over to the track and I'm on my back looking at the sky, trying to pretend I'm in the country, but I can't, because even grass in the city feels hard as sidewalk, and there's just no pretending you are anywhere but in a "concrete jungle" as my grandfather says.

The twenty-yard dash takes all of two minutes cause most of the little kids don't know no better than to run off the track or run the wrong way or run smack into the fence and fall down and cry. One little kid, though, has got the good sense to run straight for the white ribbon ahead so he wins. Then the second-graders line up for the thirty-yard dash and I don't even bother to turn my head to watch cause Raphael Perez always wins. He wins before he even begins by psyching the runners, telling them they're going to trip on their shoelaces and fall on their faces or lose their shorts or something, which he doesn't really have to do since he is very fast, almost as fast as I am. After that is the forty-yard dash which I used to run when I was in first grade. Raymond is hollering from the swings cause he knows I'm about to do my thing cause the man on the loudspeaker has just announced the fifty-yard dash, although he might just as well be giving a recipe for angel food cake cause you can hardly make out what he's saying for the static. I get up and slip off my sweat pants and then I see Gretchen standing at the starting line, kicking her legs out like a pro. Then as I get into place I see that ole Raymond is on line on the other side of the fence, bending down with his fingers on the ground just like he knew what he was doing. I was going to yell at him but then I didn't. It burns up your energy to holler.

Every time, just before I take off in a race, I always feel like I'm in a dream, the kind of dream you have when you're sick with fever and feel all hot and weightless. I dream I'm flying over a sandy beach in the early morning sun, kissing the leaves of the trees as I fly by. And there's always the smell of apples, just like in the country when I was little and used to think I was a choo-choo train, running through the fields of corn and chugging up the hill to the orchard. And all the time I'm dreaming this, I get lighter and lighter until I'm flying over the beach again, getting blown through the sky like a feather that weighs nothing at all. But once I spread my fingers in the dirt and crouch over the Get on Your Mark, the dream goes and I am solid again and am telling myself, Squeaky you must win, you must win, you are the fastest thing in the world, you can even beat your father up Amsterdam if you really try. And then I feel my weight coming back just behind my knees then down to my feet then into the earth and the pistol shot explodes in my blood and I am off and weightless again, flying past the other runners, my arms pumping up and down and the whole world is quiet except for the crunch as I zoom over the gravel in the track. I glance to my left and there is no one. To the right, a blurred Gretchen, who's got her chin jutting out as if it would win the race all by itself. And on the other side of the fence is Raymond with his arms down to his side and the palms tucked up behind him, running in his very own style, and it's the first time I ever saw that and I almost stop to watch my brother Raymond on his first run. But the white ribbon is bouncing toward me and I tear past it, racing into the distance till my feet with a mind of their own start digging up footfuls of dirt and brake me short. Then all the kids standing on the side pile on me, banging me on the back and slapping my head with their May Day programs, for I have won again and everybody on 151st Street can walk tall for another year.

"In first place . . ." the man on the loudspeaker is clear as a bell now. But then he pauses and the loud-speaker starts to whine. Then static. And I lean down to catch my breath and here comes Gretchen walking back, for she's overshot the finish line too, huffing and puffing with her hands on her hips taking it slow, breathing in steady time like a real pro and I sort of like her a little for the first time. "In first place . . ." and then three or four voices get all mixed up on the loudspeaker and I dig my sneaker into the grass and stare at Gretchen who's staring back, we both wondering just who did win. I can hear old Beanstalk arguing with the man on the loudspeaker and then a few others running their mouths about what the stopwatches say. Then I hear Raymond yanking at the fence to call me and I wave to shush him, but he keeps rattling the fence like a gorilla in a cage like in them gorilla movies, but then like a dancer or something he starts climbing up nice and easy but very fast. And it occurs to me, watching how smoothly he climbs hand over hand and remembering how he looked running with his arms down to his side and with the wind pulling his mouth back and his teeth showing and all, it occurred to me that Raymond would make a very fine runner. Doesn't he always keep up with me on my trots? And he surely knows how to breathe in counts of seven cause he's always doing it at the dinner table, which drives my brother George up the wall. And I'm smiling to beat the band cause if I've lost this race, or if me and Gretchen tied, or even if I've won, I can always retire as a runner and begin a whole new career as a coach with Raymond as my champion. After all, with a little more study I can beat Cynthia and her phony self at the spelling bee. And if I bugged my mother, I could get piano lessons and become a star. And I have a big rep as the baddest thing around. And I've got a roomful of ribbons and medals and awards. But what has Raymond got to call his own?

So I stand there with my new plans, laughing out loud by this time as Raymond jumps down from the fence and runs over with his teeth showing and his arms down to the side, which no one before him has quite mastered as a running style. And by the time he comes over I'm jumping up and down so glad to see him—my brother Raymond, a great runner in the family tradition. But of course everyone thinks I'm jumping up and down because the men on the loudspeaker have finally gotten themselves together and compared notes and are announcing "In first place— Miss Hazel Elizabeth Deborah Parker." (Dig that.) "In second place—Miss Gretchen P. Lewis." And I look over at Gretchen wondering what the "P" stands for. And I smile. Cause she's good, no doubt about it. Maybe she'd like to help me coach Raymond; she obviously is serious about running, as any fool can see. And she nods to congratulate me and then she smiles. And I smile. We stand there with this big smile of respect between us. It's about as real a smile as girls can do for each other, considering we don't practise real smiling every day, you know, cause maybe we too busy being flowers or fairies or strawberries instead of being honest and worthy of respect . . . you know . . . like being people.

# How I Write

Toni Cade Bambara

There's no particular routine to my writing, nor have any two stories come to me the same way. I'm usually working on five or six things at a time; that is, I scribble a lot in bits and pieces and generally pin them together with a working title. The actual sit-down work is still weird to me. I babble along, heading I think in one direction, only to discover myself tugged in another, or sometimes I'm absolutely snatched into an alley. I write in longhand or what kin and friends call deranged hieroglyphics. I begin on long, yellow paper with a juicy ballpoint if it's one of those 6/8 bop pieces. For slow, steady, watch-the-voice-kid, don't-let-the-mask-slip-type pieces, I prefer short, fat-lined white paper and an ink pen. I usually work it over and beat it up and sling it around the room a lot before I get to the typing stage. I hate to type—hate, hate—so things get cut mercilessly at that stage. I stick the thing in a drawer or pin it on a board for a while, maybe read it to someone or a group, get some feedback, mull it over, and put it aside. Then, when an editor calls me to say, "Got anything?" or I find the desk cluttered, or some reader sends a letter asking, "You still breathing?" or I need some dough, I'll very studiously sit down, edit, type, and send the damn thing out before it drives me crazy.

# THE
# WILD
# GOOSE

Ernest Buckler

I've never stopped missing my brother Jeff.

I'm all right; and then I pick up the rake he mended so perfectly for me where the handle went into the bow; or I come across where he'd scratched the threshing count on the barn door, with one of those clumsy fives of his in it; or it's time for someone to make the first move for bed; or some winter dusk when the sun's drawing water down beyond the frozen marshes—do you know that time of day? It's as if your heart slips into low gear.

(I'm glad Jeff can't hear me. But I don't know, maybe he wouldn't think it sounded soft. Just because he never *said* anything like that himself—you can't go by that.)

I always feel like telling something about him then. I don't know, if I can tell something to show people what he was really like it seems to help.

The wild goose flew over this evening. The sky was full of grey clouds. It looked as if it was worried about something. I could tell about Jeff and the wild goose. I never have.

It really started the afternoon before. We went hunting about four o'clock. I was fourteen and he was sixteen.

You'd never know we were brothers. You could tell exactly how he was going to look as a man, and I looked like a child that couldn't make up his mind *what* shape his face would take on later. He could lift me and my load (though he'd never once glance my way if I tackled anything beyond my strength—trying to lead a steer that was tough in the neck, or putting a cordwood butt on top of the pile, or anything). But I always seemed the older, somehow. He always seemed to—well, look up to me or something, it didn't matter how often I was mean to him.

I could draw the sprawling back field on a piece of paper and figure out the quickest way to mow it, by algebra; but when I took the machine out on the field itself I wouldn't know exactly where to begin. Jeff could take one look at the field and know exactly where to make the first swath. That was the difference between us.

And I had a quick temper, and Jeff never lost his temper except when someone was mad at *me*.

I never saw him mad at me himself but that one day. The day was so still and the sun was so bright the leaves seemed to be breathing out kind of a yellow light before they fell to the ground. I always think there's something sort of lonesome about that, don't you?

I'm no kind of hunter. You wouldn't think I was a country boy at all.

But Jeff was. He was a wonderful shot; and the minute he stepped into the woods there was a sort of brightness and a hush in his face together, I can't describe it. It wasn't that he liked the killing part. He seemed to have a funny kind of love and respect for whatever he hunted that I didn't have at all. If I don't see any game the first half a kilometre I get to feel like I'm just walking around on a fool's errand, dragging a heavy gun along. But Jeff's spell never slacked off for a second.

You'd have to live in the country to know what hunting meant to anyone like Jeff. And to know how he rated with the grown-up men; here's just this kid, see, and he knows right where to find the game, no matter how scarce it is, and to bring it home.

Anyway, we'd hardly gone any distance at all—we were just rounding that bend in the log road where there's the bit of open swamp and then what's left of the old back orchard, before the woods start—when Jeff halted suddenly and grabbed my arm.

"What's the matter?" I said.

I guess I spoke louder than ordinary, because I was startled. I hadn't thought of having to be cautious so soon.

Jeff's gun went up, but he didn't have time for even a chance to shoot. There was a flash of the big buck's flag. He'd been standing under the farthest apple tree. Then in a single motion, like the ripple in a rope when you hold one end in your hand and whap the other against the ground, he disappeared into the thicket.

Deer will sometimes stand and watch you for minutes, still as stone. Stiller than thunder weather. Stiller than holding your breath. So still you can't believe it. They're cocked for running, but you get the feeling they weren't there before you saw them. Your eyes seem to have plucked them right out of the air. Their feet don't seem to quite rest on the ground.

But the second you speak, they're off. The human voice is like a trigger.

It would have been a sure shot for Jeff. There wasn't a twig between them. It would have been the biggest buck anyone had brought home that year. Even I felt that funny sag in the day that you get when game's been within your reach except for carelessness and now there's nothing. You just keep staring at the empty spot, as if you should have known that was the one place a deer would be.

Jeff turned to me. His eyes were so hot in his head I almost crouched.

"For God's sake," he said, "don't you know enough to keep your tongue still when you're huntin'?"

It was like a slap in the face.

The minute Jeff heard what he'd said the anger went out of him. But you'd have to live in the country to know what a funny feeling it left between us. For one hunter to tell another he'd spoiled a shot. It was as if you'd reminded someone to take off his cap inside the house.

I didn't say a word. Only in my mind. I seemed to hear my mind shouting, "You just wait. You'll see. I'll never . . . never . . ." Never what, I didn't know—but just that never, never again . . .

Jeff rumbled with a laugh, trying to put the whole thing behind us, as a joke.

"Well," he said, offhand like, "that one certainly moved fast didn't he? But we'll circle around. Maybe we'll ketch him in the choppin', what?"

I didn't say a word. I just broke down my gun and took out the cartridge, then and there. I put the cartridge into my windbreaker pocket and turned toward home.

"Ain't you comin'?" Jeff said.

"What d'ya *think*?" I said.

I glanced behind me when he'd gone on. I don't know, it always strikes me there's something sort of lonesome about seeing anyone walk away back-to. I almost changed my mind and ran and caught up with him.

But I didn't. I didn't know why I could never smooth things over with Jeff right away when I knew he was sorry. I wanted to then, but I couldn't. I had to hang on to the hurt and keep it fresh. I hated what I was doing, but there it was.

It was pitch dark when Jeff got home that night, but he didn't have any deer.

I sort of kept him away from me all the next day. I hated myself for cutting off all his clumsy feelers to make up. ("What was the algebra question you showed the teacher how to do when you was only ten?") It always kind of gets me, seeing through what anyone is trying to do like that, when they don't know you can. But I couldn't help it.

(Once Jeff picked up about fifty bags of cider apples nights after school. The day he took them into town and sold them he bought every single one of us a present. I followed him to the barn that evening when he went to tend the horse. He didn't hear me coming. He was searching under the wagon seat and shaking out all the straw around the horse. He didn't want to tell me what he was looking for, but I made him. He'd lost a five-dollar bill out of the money the man at the cider mill had given him. But he'd kept the loss to himself, not to spoil our presents. That's what he was like.)

It was just about dusk when Jeff rushed into the shop the day after I'd spoiled his shot at the deer. He almost never got so excited he forgot himself, like I did. But he was that way then.

"Git your gun, Kenny, quick," he said. "There's a flock o' *geese* lit on the marsh."

It would be hard to explain why that gave even me such a peculiar thrill. Wild geese had something—well, sort of mystic—about them.

When the geese flew south in the fall, high in the sky, people would run outdoors and watch them out of sight. And when they turned back to the house again they'd have kind of a funny feeling. The geese seemed to be about the most—distant, sort of—thing in the world. In every way. You couldn't picture them on the ground, like a normal bird. Years and years ago Steve Hammond had brought one down, and it was still the first thing anyone told about him to a stranger. People said, "He shot a wild goose once," in the same tone they'd say of some famous person they'd seen, "I was close enough to touch him."

I was almost as excited as Jeff. But I kept rounding up my armful, pretending the geese didn't matter much to me one way or the other.

"Never mind the *wood*," Jeff said. He raced into the house for his gun.

I piled up a full load before I went into the house and dropped it into the box. It must have almost killed him to wait for me. But he did.

"Come on. Come on," he urged, as we started down across the field. "And put in a ball cartridge. We'll never git near enough fer shot to carry."

I could see myself hitting that small a target with a ball cartridge! But I did as he said.

When we got to the railroad cut, we crawled on our bellies, so we could use the embankment the rails ran along as a blind. We peeked over it, and there they were.

They were almost the length of the marsh away, way down in that mucky spot where the men cut sods for the dike, but their great white breasts looked big as pennants. They had their long black necks stretched up absolutely straight and still, like charmed cobras. They must have seen us coming down across the field.

Jeff rested the barrel of his gun on a rail. I did the same with mine. But mine was shaking so it made a clatter and I raised it higher.

"I'll count five," Jeff whispered. "Then both fire at once." I nodded and he began to count.

"One. Two. Three . . ."

I fired.

Jeff's shot came a split second afterward. He gave me a quick inquisitive glance, but he didn't say a word about me firing before the count was up.

He threw out his empty shell and loaded again. But the geese had already lifted, as if all at once some spring in the ground had shot them into the air. They veered out over the river.

All but one, that is. Its white breast was against the ground and we didn't see it in the blur of wings until its own wings gave one last flutter.

"We got one!" Jeff shouted. "Well, I'll be. . . . We got one!"

He bounded down across the marsh. I came behind, walking.

When I got there he was stroking the goose's soft down almost tenderly. It was only a dead bird to me now, but to him it seemed like some sort of mystery made flesh and shape. There was hardly a mark on it. The bullet had gone through his neck, fair as a die.

Then Jeff made a funny face. He handed the goose to me. He was sort of grinning.

"Here," he said. "Carry her. She's yours. That was some shot, mister."

"Mine?" I said.

"Sure." He looked half sheepish. I'm a hell of a hunter, I am. I had two ball cartridges in this here pocket, see, and two shot in this one." He put his hand into the first pocket and held out two ball cartridges in his palm. "I guess I got rattled and put the shot in my gun instidd o' the ball. You know how far shot'd carry. It was you that got him, no doubt about *that*."

I carried the goose home.

It didn't mean much to me, but he didn't know that. He could only go by what it would have meant to him, if he'd been the one to carry it home. I knew what he was thinking. This would wipe out what I'd done yesterday. And the men wouldn't look at me now the way they looked at a bookworm but the way they looked at a hunter.

I'm glad that for once I had the decency to pretend I was as excited and proud as he'd thought I'd be. I'm glad I didn't say a word—not then—to let him know I saw through the trick.

For I knew it was a trick. I knew I hadn't shot the goose. While he was counting I'd felt that awful passion to wreck things which always got into me when I was still smarting over something. I had fired before he did, on purpose. Way over their heads, to scare them.

The day Jeff went away we sort of stuck around close to each other, but we couldn't seem to find anything to say.

I went out to the road to wait for the bus with him. Jeff had on his good clothes. They never looked right on him. When I dressed up I looked different, but Jeff never did. I don't know why, but every time I saw Jeff in his good clothes I felt sort of—well, like *defending* him or something.

The bus seemed to take a long time coming. He was going away in the army. He'd be with guys who were twice as much like him as I was, but just the same I knew he'd rather be with me than with them. I don't know, buses are such darned lonesome things, somehow.

When the bus was due, and I knew we only had left what few minutes it might be late, I tried to think of something light to say, the way you're supposed to.

The only thing that came into my mind was that day with the goose. It was a funny thing to bring up all of a sudden. But now we were a couple of years older I thought I could make something out of it to amuse him. Besides, when someone's going away you have the feeling that you ought to get everything straight between you. You hardly ever can, but you get that feeling.

"You shot the goose that day," I said, "didn't you?"

He nodded.

I'd never have opened my fool mouth if I'd known what was going to happen then. I'd felt sort of still and bad, but I hadn't felt like crying. How was I to know that the minute I mentioned that day the whole thing would come back so darn plain? I'd have died rather than have Jeff see my face break up like that.

But on the other hand, I don't care how soft it sounds, I'm sort of glad I did, now. He didn't look embarrassed, to see me cry. He looked so darned surprised— and then all at once he looked happier than I believe I ever saw him.

That was Jeff. He'll never come back. I don't even know which Korean hill it was—the telegram didn't say. But when I tell anything about him like this I seem to feel that *somewhere* he's sort of, I don't know, half-smiling— like he used to when we had some secret between us we'd never even discussed. I feel that if I could just make him absolutely clear to everyone he wouldn't really be dead at all. Tonight when the geese flew over I wished I knew how to write a book about him.

The geese didn't light this time. They never have since that day. I don't know, I always think there's something lonesome about wild geese.

But I feel better now. Do you know how it is?

# DO YOU
# REALLY THINK
# IT'S FAIR?

Norma Fox Mazer

---

**W**ell, here I am.

What? I'm Sara Gorelick! Didn't you ask me to come to your office? Mrs. Teassle *said*—Oh. No, I guess we haven't met before. But I know who *you* are. So, what's up?

You've heard about me? I didn't know I was famous. The *famous* Sara Gorelick! . . . What?

No, I don't want to be a movie star! A model? *No.* Well . . . a judge.

Uh-huh. You heard me right. A judge. I don't think that's so funny. What's the hilarious joke? Yes, you are too laughing at me! I know when somebody is laughing and—Look, *you* asked me to come down here. You *asked* me. That means I don't have to stay, doesn't it? I can leave, right? Because if you asked me to come to your office just to laugh at me—!

Sensitive? I'm not *sensitive*. No, that's *not* the way I

would describe myself. I'm—I'm—I'm *tough*. Okay? Now would you *please* tell me why I'm here? Which one of my teachers complained about me? Bet it was Sweetie Sorenson. It was, wasn't it? Just because I told him that assignment was dumb.

Yes, I did say that. Interview somebody who's over thirty. What does *that* mean? What's so gorgeous great about being over thirty?

It *wasn't* Mr. Sorenson who—Oh, it was, but—*what*?

A consensus of my teachers? Yes, I know what that means.

Where? Where does it say that about me? Has become unruly and— Why can't I see the rest of that? Privileged material? That's just another way of saying you don't want me to see it. Why do grown-ups lie to kids? Yes, they do. All the time. Sure, I can prove it.

They lied in the hospital. They said Jayne would come out of it. Would live. They said it. Two doctors—

An honest mistake?

Oh, it's always a mistake when you're grown up. If you're a kid, it's murder, right? If a kid had been driving that car . . .

You know what the judge said? He said it could have happened to anyone. That's a lie. He said it wasn't the driver's fault. No charges. Because the sun was in his eyes, and Jayne ran out into the street. That's all lies. He didn't say anything about the man drinking. And Jayne *didn't run out*. She looked both ways. Eight years old—she's not *dumb*.

She *looked*, and that man, that driver—we shouted at him. All of us. We saw it. We saw Jayne running out after the ball. We saw the car coming and coming, and we all started shouting and screaming. Stop! Stop! Stop!

No, I'm not crying. *No*. I am *not* crying. I don't cry.

What?

Because I don't want to, that's why! Why should
I cry?

*You* want me to cry? What business is it of yours if
I—What are you, weird?

Yes, sure, McClure, that's a *good example* of the way
I talk to everyone!

Yes, I know why I'm here. You want to brainwash
me. Make me polite and nice and good. Good little girl.
Make goo-goo eyes at people. Or maybe you'd just like to
put a piece of tape across my mouth! Look, I'm going
now. I don't want to stay here. There's no law says I have
to stay, is there? Swell, Mr. Fell! *Good*-bye!

You wanted to see me again? So what's new, Mr.
Blue? Do you remember my name this time? Sara, without an *H*. Oh, I'm feelin' just fine, Mr. Cline, how about
you?

Stop spinning around and sit down?

Okay, I'm down. Well, what's it all about? Here I am,
and let's get it over with.

What?

I don't have much to say about it, do I? I mean, you
asked me, but I *have* to come, don't I? Anyway, I don't
care. I'm cool, Mr. Ghoul. I get out of Music this way.

Sure, I can guess why you asked me to come back.
That report—unruly Sara Garlic!

Garlic? Joke. Family joke.

How do I feel about my family? Fine.

How do I feel about school? Blaaagh!

How do I feel about *you?* You really want to know?
Or you want me to lie? You want me to lie, don't you?
Nobody asks a question like that and wants the truth.

*You* do?

Uh, okay, you asked for it. How I feel about you—uh, nothing special. You know, shrug. Yawn. Blah, blah, blah, that's your job, isn't it? Talk, talk, talk. You want me to leave now? You want to put me in a corner? You want to send me to detention?

What? I can say *anything*, and it's okay? You won't take it personally? What if I mean it personally?

You still won't take it personally.

Uh, great. What are you, nuts? I mean, that is *really* weird. Koo. Koo.

Why you asked me to come here? That's easy. To braid my brains. To mangle my mind. To . . .

No, I don't think you're a shrink. You're a guidance counselor. A psychologist, right? What word? Psychologist? What's the big deal about knowing— What? The difference between a psychologist and a psychiatrist? One has to be a doctor. You didn't go to medical school, did you?

What? Well, I read a lot. Everyone in my family reads a lot—my mother, my father, my sis—

We all like to read, okay! Is that such a big *D* deal?

What was I going to say about my sister? Nothing!

No, I was *not*, I didn't even mention her name. Forget it! I don't want to talk about her.

What? That's one of the tasks you and I—I don't get this. What do you mean, a *task*?

*Yes*, I know what a *task* is.

Talking about my sister is a task? Is that why I'm here? Then maybe I just better leave. Because I'm not going to talk about her. No, I'm not. And I'm not going to cry, either. You have got some very mixed-up, crazy ideas. I thought you got me here because I'm giving my teachers trouble and . . .

No, I don't think there's anything wrong with crying.

If that's what you want to do, be my guest. I'll bring you a box of Kleenex. Just, *I* don't want to. Can you understand that? You dig, Mr. Fig? Don't want to cry. Do not want to cry. No cry. Sara no want water to come from her eye. Is clear?

Clear as water? Very funny, ha ha. Dr. I. C. Brains has big sense of humor. Can I go now?

What?

No, oh, no. Oh, no, oh, no, it-doesn't-have-anything-to-do-with-Jayne! I told you. I AM NOT GOING TO TALK ABOUT HER.

*Yes*, I'll talk about my family. I don't see what difference it makes to you, though. My dad's an electrician, my mom's an RN. Okay? Enough?

*Yes*, my mom likes working, don't you?

Uh-huh, Community Hospital on Greene Street. Right, same street we live on, but the other end, way down. No, she mostly rides her bike there. My father needs the car.

What?

*Yes*, that's my whole family. My father, my mother, and me.

You can't see my face? That's because I'm not looking at you.

Because I *feel* like sitting this way. Does a person have to sit a special way in your office? Next time I'll wear my T-shirt with Wonder Woman on the back so you can look at her. No, I'm not getting upset! Do you want to ask me anything else, or can I go back to my class now?

No, there's nothing I want to talk about!

I just told you. I'M NOT UPSET. I'M FINE. I'm mellow, Mr. Bellow. All right, all right, I'll come back. Next week, yes, okay. Next week.

Sara Sass reporting in, sir!

Nice shirt you're wearing. Do you always sit that same exact way? With your fingers together? Maybe I should sit behind the desk and you could sit right here in the hot seat. You need a little head shrinking? A bit of brain unkinking? Sara will save you. Is that a smile I see, or a frown?

Oh—neither. Do you think I'm being fresh? Rude? Obnoxious? Unruly?

Won't answer, will you? I can say anything right? But that doesn't mean *you* stop thinking, does it? Bet you think I'm a weird fresh brat! That's why I'm down here. Right? Freshness and general messing up. General Messing Up reporting to Sergeant Scrambler. Were you in the army, Private? Is that why it says on your door—

What?

Am I going to settle d—

I thought you *wanted* me to talk. Just trying to please, talking up a breeze. Last time you were practically *begging* me—

Do I know—*Yes*, I know what *appropriate* means. Gotta get down to business, huh? Oh, right, right, must get on with our tasks. Where's the mop and pail? Or do you want me to wash the windows? Or should I clean your desk, that's a *mess*, wow, my mother wouldn't stand for—

What?

You don't think we're going to get anything done this time if I—

Well, I don't care, Mr. Hair. It doesn't matter. You're the one who keeps asking me to come here. Am I driving you up a wall? That's what Mrs. Clendon said to me. Sara, you're driving me up a wall! Oh. You know about that. Were you shocked? Were you surprised? Were you real mad?

Well, because you're supposed to be working miracles on me, aren't you? Making me behave. Be a good little Sara.

No, I don't dislike Mrs. Clendon. She's pretty nice for a teacher. Then why do I—I don't know. Just some devil or something gets in me, I guess.

I know.

I *know* that.

I know I was never a troublemaker. Well, there's always a first time, ha ha. Who cares anyway? It doesn't matter.

Why do I keep saying *what*? That it doesn't matter? Must be because it's true. It doesn't matter.

*What* doesn't matter?

Nothing.

Nothing matters. Everything is all crazy and weird. The *world* is weird. You know? It really is. That's what I think. The world is weird and unfair. It really just *stinks*.

Sure, I think that. *Sure*, I do!

No, those are not tears in my eyes! I wish you wouldn't keep saying that! How many times do I have to tell you the same thing? I do not *cry*, mister. I-do-not-cry. I do *not* cry. I do not, I do not, I do not!


Hello.

No, I don't mind that the office is dark. I like to be someplace dark when it's raining outside.

What?

Quiet? I can be quiet, too. I'm not a freak, you know. I'm not just a big loudmouth.

You never said— But isn't that what you were thinking?

No? Well—if you say so.

Sure, we can talk. What do you want to say?

Yes, I have friends.

Best friend? Callie Gerstein, I guess.

Naturally I talk to her. Was she—? Yes, she was there the day Jayne—A whole bunch of us from the street. We were playing softball and— Do I have to tell you that all over again?

Did Jayne have friends? Yes, *sure*. Well, I had to watch her, that's why she was with—

Look. Is this some kind of test or something?

Well, the way you're asking things. They did that to Jayne once. Sneaked a test on her when she was in first grade. Asked her a million questions and then wanted to skip her to third.

No. My mother wouldn't let them. Was I—Yes, I was glad. That would have put her practically in my grade. Who wants their bratty little sister—

Sure, she was a brat! A big brat! And she always had to hang around with me. Drag! Double drag! *Because* my mother *works*. Somebody has to look after—I mean, somebody *had* to—Why are you asking me all these dumb questions?

What? *Yes*, I know what ground rules are.

Yes, I'm listening. I don't have to look into your big baby blues every *second* to listen.

I *know* you're just trying to do your job— All right, all right, I'll *try*. But if *your* ground rule is for me to answer the questions, *my* ground rule is for you to stop asking if I know what every other word means! Yes, you *do*. What am I angry about? Nothing! Who says I'm mad? I don't care what you say it sounds like, *I'm not mad about anything*. I want another ground rule! You don't tell me what I am! Like angry, or un-ruly, or—

*Yes*, I'll answer your questions, I *said* I would. I keep my word. Do you?

Okay! It's a deal, Mr. Seal. Go ahead. Shoot. Ask me anything . . . Jayne? Tell you about Jayne? Do we have to—

Okay, okay, I know. You ask, I answer.

Jayne. She was my sister. That 's all.

A memory? Any memory? Just start anywhere? I don't know where to— I told you, she was a brat, a real pest, a baby who bugged me. Made me crazy sometimes. Like how? Like when I got a bike for my birthday. I was nine. Thought I was so grown up. They gave me a two-wheeler. Right, Jayne was four. She had a trike of her own. But she had to learn to ride *my* two-wheeler, or *nothing*. She must have fallen a million times. Skinned her knees, bloodied up her hands. Almost knocked out a tooth.

Everybody told her, *Quit*, you're too little.

She didn't quit. She learned to ride. The seat was too high for her. She didn't care, she stood up on the pedals. *No*, I wasn't *proud* of her. What for? After that I had to share my bike with her. Every time *I* wanted to ride, *she'd* be on it. My mother would say, Share and share alike.

No, they didn't. Said she was too young. Said bikes were too expensive. Said when she got older, and more careful.

I don't know. Maybe next year they would have.

What? It was a *Raleigh*. She messed it up. Full of scratches. Dents. She banged it up a million times. Never used the kick stand, just let the bike drop on the ground. She never took care of anything. In our room— Yes, same room. We live in an apartment—two bedrooms. I keep begging my parents, Let me sleep in the hall! My mother says, Nothing doing.

Why do I want to—Because Jayne is such a slob.

Never picks up her clothes or books or—Can we talk about something else? Is the time up yet? I'm—I'm sort of tired . . . don't want to talk anymore.

Wednesday? All right. Ten o'clock? Keen, jelly bean. I'll be here.


Here I am again.

Yes, I'm ready. Yes, I remember our ground rules. Do you? You've got more to remember than I do.

What?

Go through my *anger*? I told you I'm not—

You want me to understand *what*?

The *steps* of sorrow? Ah, ha ha. Where do they lead to? Is it just one flight? Can I run up them, or do I have to walk slowly, like a lady? That's what Mrs. Christmas told me yesterday. Sara Gorelick, ladies don't run, they *walk*. What'd I do? I laughed. What would you do if someone—Oh, it's no good asking you, anyway, guys never get told stuff like that. Lester Coleman, gentlemen don't run, they *walk*. Can you hear it?

We're getting off the subject?

Oh, right, right, back to the steps of sorrow. Take 'em two at a time, gang.

Look! There's no rule that I can't make jokes. Lots of things are jokes. Oh, I forgot, you like tears better than laughter, right?

I'm being recalcitrant? Wow-ee, that's a mouthful. Uh, uh, uh, can't ask if I know what it means! Ha! But—I'll tell you this. If you were my dad, instead of that you would have said, Sara, you're acting like a regular little *jackass*. Ha, guessed it right, didn't I?

Sure, I'm in good spirits today. The sun is shining and I ate my Rice Krispies this morning. Yippee. Only pretty soon, if I have to go on listening to this lecture about the three steps of sorrow, I might feel like throwing up my snap, crackle, and pop.

Hey. Did I make you feel bad?

I didn't mean anything. Just joking around.

Oh. You're just thinking of where to start this morning. Whew. Had me fooled for a minute there. I thought the talking question machine was running down. No such luck, huh?

Tell you about Jayne? Again?

All right, *again*!

What did she look like. Skinny, sort of dirty blond hair, freckles. Right, right, we don't look anything alike. She's like my mom, I'm like my dad. Pretty? I don't know. Cute, I guess. My mom would send me to the store for milk and bread. And Jayne would say, Can I come with you, Sara? Can I come with you, Sara? Just to shut her up, I'd say, Okay! She talked so much. Just like you. Blah, blah, blah, she never ran out of stuff to talk about. You think *I* have a big mouth . . .

People would look at her and say, Your little sister is adorable. Those freckles! And they'd smile and pat her on the head. She was real jumpy about her head being patted. One time a man in the supermarket said, Hello, little girl. And he goes to her head, *pat pat pat*. It really set her off. Leave my head *alone*, she yelled.

She just couldn't stand the feeling of being bonked on the head. Nobody ever asked her. They just figured, She's a kid, so that gives them the right to smack her on the head.

Yes, I think adults run the world. Don't you? Kids don't have anything to say about anything . . .

Maybe we *could* do a better job. Maybe we'd be a whole lot more *fair*. What do I mean by that? Can't you figure it out? Give you an example? Sure! That man who ran into Jayne. What happened to *him*? He didn't even have his license taken away. And he was drinking. Drunk. Yes, he *was*. I smelled it on him. He got out of his big car. Big black Chrysler. Jayne was lying there in the road, and I smelled it on him. I smelled it on him!

What?

Yes, I know. I know they said it wasn't his fault. But they didn't even say about him drinking when he went to court. Do you think that's fair? Yes, I was there. We all were. Me, Mom, and Dad. We heard the judge. We heard everything. They didn't ask me, no. Because I'm just a kid, maybe. Or maybe because of who he is, his name—

What's that got to do with—?

Are you *kidding*? His name is the same as Senator— What? He's his *brother*. That's right, his brother, and he should be in jail. I would have put him in jail. When I'm a judge, I won't care who anybody is. I won't care if the *President's* brother comes in my court. I'll just listen to the facts and I'll make everybody tell the truth!

There's the bell. Good-bye!

Hi.

No, I don't feel like sitting down today.

There's no place to walk here. How come your office is so small? It looks like they made it out of a closet. They *did*. This really used to be a closet? Tacky!

So what's your question today?

Do I dream about Jayne?

Boy, you know how to pick 'em. I bet you put in lots of time thinking up these questions. Am I going to ans— Okay, okay. Answer: I don't know. Maybe. Sometimes. I don't want to talk about that.

All right! I'll keep my promise! What do you want to know? A dream I had about her? Okay, I dreamed we were on a horse together. Satisfied?

You're not.

All . . . right. I'll tell you more. A big white horse. And we were galloping across a field. . . . I don't know what kind of field! Does it matter? A field, just a field, ordinary, with flowers and bees and things.

I don't *know* why I dreamed that. You just dream things. No, we never had a horse. Jayne wanted one, though. She was horse-crazy. Her side of the room was all covered with horse pictures. Once, when she was about six, she begged Mom and Dad to get her a horse. My mother said even if we could afford it, which we couldn't, where would we put it?

And Jayne says, In the backyard.

What a dodo. Our backyard is just about big enough for the clothesline.

So, next, Jayne says, I'll keep him in the bedroom. I'll get a pony and he can go at the foot of my bed.

We were all laughing. Zowie! Did that make Jayne mad. Her eyes are sort of greenish, and when she gets mad, they go all dark, and then her face gets bunchy and red, and looks like her freckles are going to jump right off her skin.

My mother says, Someday your face is going to freeze like that, Jayne, and then you're going to be one strange-looking kid. And Jayne goes, Ha! Ha! Very funny! Boy, that's really funny! And then my father gets into the act. Don't be fresh to your mother.

And Jayne goes Ha! Ha! again, right in his face. Which is big dumbness. You can say lots of stuff to my mother. But my father—no. So he gets mad and gives her a whup on the behind.

No, she didn't cry. You couldn't make that kid cry. Not that way. She'd cry if she found a dead animal. One time she found a mouse that a cat killed. It was stiff, with blood on its neck. Jayne picks it right up and puts her hands around it, like she's going to warm it up and make it live again.

I go, Come on, Jayne, it's dead. Put it down. It's full of germs.

And she goes, Listen, Sara, *listen*. I can feel its *heart*. And she wants to bring it home and take care of it. Yeah, she did it. Sneaked it into the house and kept it for two days until it started to stink and my mom found it.

*Sometimes* I could persuade her to do things but mostly, no. Nobody could. She's just stubborn. Like the time Mom cut my hair. Wanted to cut Jayne's hair, too. Oh no, you don't, Jayne says. Oh, no, you don't.

And she's backing away, holding her hair like Mom was going to chop it off right to the roots. So Mom and I both try telling her how cute she'll look.

She says, Who cares! I want my hair!

Then we say stuff like how much easier it will be to comb and all that. And Jayne says, I love my hair!

And she runs into the bathroom and locks the door and won't come out until Mom promises, sacred word of honor, not to cut her hair.

My father says we all let her get her own way too much. I sure agree with him! That brat can be stubborn, and *dumb*, too.

Like *what*?

Like once she jumped into a lake from a second-story window. Because somebody dared her. My mom said she could have been ki—Is that dumb enough for you? Can we change the subject now?

Games? Sure we played games together. Just dumb kid stuff. You don't want to hear—

You do.

You are the most curious person I ever met. You are a real big *B* brain picker.

Games. Right.

Umm . . . one we played was lying on our beds and walking our legs up the wall to see who could go the highest. Jayne always won, because she would walk herself up until only the back of her head was on the bed.

You want *more*? Whew. You're never satisfied. Okay, we played our-favorite-room—telling about this room we'd have if someone left us a million dollars and we could buy anything we wanted. Uh-huh, Jayne always puts a horse in her room. It's one of her favorite games. She goes, Can I go first, Sara? I have to go first, Sara! Sara, if you don't let me go first—! Bugs me *crazy*.

What? *What*?

There's some *confusion* in me—? I don't know what you're talking about.

I *what*? . . . Sometimes I talk as if Jayne is still alive? I don't know what you mean. I'm just telling you things. You ask, I tell. Like I said, Keen, jelly bean.

Why are you so picky anyway? What if I do talk about her as if—

Yes, I hear you. I'm *listening*. I understand. I'm not stupid! You think I don't want to face facts.

No, *I* didn't say I don't want to face facts. I said that's what *you*—Oh, what's the use? Forget it!

No, I AM NOT GETTING MAD. AND I AM NOT GETTING UPSET. Do you have to keep ASKING me that?

Are you kidding? Mad because Jayne died. Mad at *Jayne*? That would be super dumbness, wouldn't it?

If you want to know if I'm mad at anybody, it's you, Mr. *B*. Brain Picker. Yes, *you* make me mad. You make me see red, white, and blue! How mad do you make me?

THIS mad! THIS mad! THIS MAD THIS MAD THIS MAD THIS MAD!

What? Did it feel good banging my fists on your desk? Why should it feel good? I hurt my knuckles. My throat is sore. *No*, it's all *right*. Leave me alone. Can I go now? You don't want to talk to me anymore, do you?

That's true, Mr. Rue. I don't want to talk to *you* anymore. How much of this do you think I can stand? Nothing personal. You said I should say what I felt, honestly. So I'm saying it. GOOD-BYE! And if I never see you again it'll be too soon for me!

Heigh ho, Mr. Snow.
You mad at me?
I didn't think so.
I'm right on time today.
Yes, it's a beautiful day. Uh-huh, very warm. No, I don't mind sitting down. Here on the windowsill okay? I *like* it better, is why. If you turn around . . . see, no big desk between us. More *equal*—

Why did I use that word? What word? *Equal*? I don't know. Just said, More equal.

What does it remind me of? Oh, boy, picking my brains again.

Oh, okay, I'll humor you. One and one *equals* two. More? Great.

Are-you-*equal*-to-the-task-we-are-all-created-*equal*-in-the-eyes-of-God. What's this all about, anyway?

Am *I* equal to the task of saying Jayne is de—

Why should I say that? What *difference* does it make? I know she's—I *know* what happened—

I *told* you . . . I can say it if I *want* to!

I-just-don't-want-to.

What? You want me to say it anyway? Just to

prove—Big deal! My sister is . . .

*Why do you want me to say it?*

No, I am *not* afraid to say it! MY SISTER IS DEAD.

There! Are you satisfied now? God! *I hate you.* No, don't touch me! Leave me alone! *Leave me alone.* I'm going now. I'm going!


Hello?

Should I, ah, come in?

Hi. . . .

I'm quieter than usual? No, I'm not. I'm like this lots of times. I just haven't got anything special to say.

I've been feeling—okay . . . Sure . . . okay . . .

What?

Do I realize . . . *ten minutes?* I haven't said anything for ten minutes? Just been sitting here?

Daydreaming, I guess.

No, nothing special. Just about something that happened once. You probably don't want to hear. I mean, you're more morbid. You like to tune in on funerals and accidents and . . .

Now I sound more like myself? Old Sassy Sara? How come you smile when you say that?

Oh. Uh. Well, I like you, too. But don't go getting a big swelled head about it. You're not the only grown-up in the entire world that I like, you know!

And I don't even like you that much, anyway.

Oh, back to *that.*

It was something that happened on Halloween. The Parks Department had a fair. You wouldn't be interest— You would be. Okay, if you *insist.*

Well, there was this fair, like I said. And I wanted to go, and Mom said I had to take Jayne. I didn't like that. Callie and I wanted to go alone. We already took Jayne out trick-or-treating. She was seven—it was last year. She says, Oh, please take me, Sara! I'll be good! I promise. I'll give you my stuffed kangaroo.

Big deal. Just what I wanted, her stuffed kangaroo that she still chewed on when she sulked.

Yes, I took her. I had to. There was this huge crowd in the park. Booths selling popcorn and candy apples, and a beauty contest booth, and this one place where you went in, got a slimy trickle down your back, and then a skeleton jumped out at you. We went in there. It was crazy. We were screaming and laughing. We did some more stuff, but all Jayne wanted was to go over to the greased pole. I had to yell at her every two minutes to stick with me and Callie.

Then one time I turned around and she was gone. The greased pole, naturally. Because they promised anybody who climbed to the top a pony. Free.

Uh-huh, they greased the flagpole in the middle of the park.

Oh, sure, you could get your legs around the pole, and start climbing, but not far. You'd slide right down, 'cause you couldn't get a grip with your hands. And meanwhile you get covered from head to toe with grease!

But that's where Jayne was. No, not watching. *Climbing*. She'd go up and she'd slide down. And she'd go up again. I yelled at her to come down. She didn't even look at me. Just kept trying. And this humongous bunch of people are watching her. Jayne, come down, I yelled again. And she yells back, Sara, I got to climb this pole!

And she's wriggling up like a monkey. And sliding down.

She just kept trying. And trying. I don't know how long. A *long* time.

People were clapping for her, saying stuff like, Go, Freckles! Way to go, kid! Stuff like that.

You wouldn't believe what she looked like when I finally dragged her home. Jeans, shirt, face, hair, arms—everything, *total* grease.

You dumb kid, I said. I'm yanking her along by the hand. Why didn't you come down when I called you? Wail till Mom sees you!

And she goes, I could've climbed that pole if you didn't make me come down, Sara!

*Make her*! I go, You are stupid. Nobody could climb that pole. Why do you think they said they'd give a free pony?

Shut up, she goes. Sara, you're an ass! Then she sort of jumps on me, gets me all greasy, too, and pounds on me and yells, Shut up, Sara! Shut up, Sara! Keeps saying that. Shut up, Sara! Shut up, Sara!

Then we get home, and my *mother* yells at me. I told you to watch her, Sara! I thought I could depend on you! I thought you had sense!

She got Jayne cleaned up and we went to bed. After a while Jayne goes, Sara!

And I go, Don't talk to me!

And she goes, My feet are cold. Can I get in bed with you? And before I can say anything, she's out of her bed and in my bed, pushing me over and strangling me with her arms around my neck. Her hair still stinks of grease. So I shove her away. But I can't shove her off me. So we fall asleep that way, and—and—

*What?*

*I am not crying.* Don't look at me!

No, I don't need tissues. Keep your stupid tissues. Why did you get me talking about—Oh, *no*.

All right, I'm *crying*. Are you happy now? You made me—Just leave me . . . *just leave me* . . . Jayne . . . she left me . . . oh, no, no, no, no . . . no . . . noooo . . .

Hi. You ready for me?

The last session? After this you don't think I have to come back unless I feel like talking? I always feel like talking. But not to you, ha ha.

Oh. You're still being serious. Right. Question. Shoot.

How did I feel after I cried? Do you have to be so *personal*?

All right, I'll answer your question one more time! I didn't like it. No, I didn't like crying!

You're smart. Can't you guess why? Don't you *know*?

If you cry, you could cry everything away. Everything, everything.

What do I *mean*?

I mean what I say. Everything I remember. Everything I feel. If I cry it all away, won't I forget? Yes, and then— and then Jayne will really be gone, won't she? That's my question for *you*.

Yes. Yes, yes, I know. You've said it to me. It's a fact. She's dead, I know—See, I can say it if I want to. She-is-dead. My-sister-is-dead. And I cried. You should be very happy. That's what you wanted.

No, there's no more I want to say.

Uh-huh, I guess it's good that I talked about her. If you say so. And cried. Yes. I can see your point. Yes, I'm sure you're right. I'll feel better now, yes.

Only . . .

What? I was going to say something else? Oh.

Oh, just one thing.

I can't stop thinking one thing. Do you think it's fair? That Jayne is dead? Do you really think it's fair?

# Perhaps the Trees Do Travel

Roch Carrier

There were those who had travelled like migratory birds and those who lived rooted to the earth, like trees. Some had gone very far. I remember hearing the story of a man who had gone to the place where the sky meets the earth: he'd had to bend down so he wouldn't bump his head against the sky. The man had suddenly felt lonely and he'd written to his wife. The stamp cost a thousand dollars. Some people had gone to New York; another visited a brother in Montana; my grandfather had sailed on the Atlantic Ocean; a family had migrated to Saskatchewan; and men went to cut timber in the forests of Maine or Abitibi. When these people came home in their new clothes, even the trees on the main street were a little envious of the travellers.

And there were those who had never gone away. Like old Herménégilde. He was so old he'd seen the first house being built in our village. He was old, but his mustache was still completely black. It was a huge mustache that hid his nose, his mouth, and his chin. I can still see old Herménégilde's mustache like a big black cloud over our village. Our parents used to say of him that he was healthy as a horse; all the storms of life had been unable to bend his upright, solid pride. At the end of his life he possessed nothing but a small frame house. All his children were gone. Old Herménégilde had spent his whole life without ever going outside the village limits. And he was very proud of having lived that way, rooted to the soil of our village. To indicate the full extent of his pride he would say:

"I've lived my whole life and never needed strangers!"

Old Herménégilde had never gone running off to the distant forests, he had never gone to the neighbouring villages to buy or sell animals. He'd found his wife in the village. Old Herménégilde used to say:

"The good Lord gave us everything we need to get by right here in our village! How come people have to go running off somewheres else where it ain't no better?"

He recalled a proverb written by a very old French poet and repeated it in his own way:

"The fellow next door's grass always looks a heck of a lot greener than your own."

Old Herménégilde had never been inside an automobile.

"I'm in no rush to die," he said. "I want to do it on foot, like a man."

One morning a black car longer than the one driven by Monsieur Cassidy, the undertaker, stopped with a jolt in front of old Herménégilde's house. A son he hadn't seen for a good many years got out of the car, all dressed in black, as Monsieur Cassidy usually was.

"You coming to my burial, my boy?" asked Old Herménégilde.

"No," said the son. "I came to take you on a trip."

Moving from one trade, one job to another, the son had become the private chauffeur to a businessman from Montreal; before he could ask himself what was happening, old Herménégilde, who had never been in a car before, was pushed onto the leather seat of a Cadillac that pawed the ground like a horse.

"Father," said the son, "you can't die before you see the world a little."

"I've seen everything a man needs to see," said old Herménégilde.

The son's long black car carried him off at a speed he'd never experienced. To avoid seeing that he was going beyond the village limits, old Herménégilde closed his eyes. And with his eyes closed the old man didn't see that he was driving through the neighbouring village, where a number of old men had gone to get their wives; he didn't see Mont Orignal, the highest mountain in the region; he didn't see the ten villages the black car drove through at a speed no runaway horse had ever reached. Tobie, his son, was talking, but he didn't want to listen.

"I'm your son and I know you've spent your whole life as if you were in jail. But you gotta see the world before you die and I'm the one that'll take you out of that jail. Nowadays there's no such thing as distance. My boss, he gets up in Montreal, he opens his eyes in Toronto, he eats his breakfast in New York and then comes back to Montreal to go to sleep. That's what I call living! You gotta keep up with the times. We know the world turns. And you gotta turn with it. I never stop travelling. I know the world. I know life. But you, you've never lived in modern times. It's something you gotta see."

"A man can go as far as he wants," said old Herménégilde, "but he always stays in the same pair of boots."

"I'm not what you'd call a good son," said Tobie, "but I'm the one that's gonna show you the world. That'll be one good thing I've done in my life."

So then old Herménégilde understood that he was no longer allowed to keep his eyes closed. They had entered Quebec City. In a single glance the old man took in houses taller than the church, more people in the street than for a religious procession, and cars swarming everywhere, like ants. His son drove him in front of an immense château, a real château whose name he'd heard when people talked about the rich—the Château Frontenac; then he showed him something much older than he was, older even than his late father—the houses built by the first Frenchmen.

The black car stopped in front of a large garden. Tobie helped his father get out.

"Now people won't be able to say you died without ever setting foot on the Plains of Abraham. This is where we lost our country. . . ."

And then it was time to go home. In the car, the son noticed that old Herménégilde was keeping his eyes closed.

"Father, don't shut your eyes, look at the people."

"I seen too much," said the old man, "you showed me too many things today."

As soon as the son had left old Herménégilde at his house, he hurried off again in the long black car, summoned by other journeys in the vast modern world.

For long months, behind his big black mustache and his closed eyes, old Herménégilde waited for the long black car to return.

# COMBING

Bending, I bow my head
And lay my hands upon
Her hair, combing, and think
How women do this for
Each other. My daughter's hair
Curls against the comb,
Wet and fragrant—orange
Parings. Her face, downcast,
Is quiet for one so young.

I take her place. Beneath
My mother's hands I feel
The braids drawn up tight
As a piano wire and singing,
Vinegar-rinsed. Sitting
Before the oven I hear
The orange coils tick
The early hour before school.

She combed her grandmother
Mathilda's hair using
A comb made out of bone.
Mathilda rocked her oak wood
Chair, her face downcast,
Intent on tearing rags
In strips to braid a cotton
Rug from bits of orange
And brown. A simple act,

Preparing hair. Something
Women do for each other,
Plaiting the generations.

GLADYS CARDIFF

# The Seven Ages of Life

*This excerpt, taken from Shakespeare's play*
As You Like It, *is as appropriate for today as
it was when it was written some four hundred
years ago.*

All the world's a stage,
And all the men and women merely players:[1]
They have their exits and their entrances;
And one man in his time plays many parts,
His acts being seven ages.[2] At first the infant,
Mewling[3] and puking in the nurse's arms.
And then the whining schoolboy, with his satchel,
And shining morning face, creeping like snail
Unwillingly to school. And then the lover,
Sighing like furnace, with a woeful ballad
Made to his mistress' eyebrow. Then a soldier,
Full of strange oaths, and bearded like the pard,[4]
Jealous in honor,[5] sudden and quick in quarrel,
Seeking the bubble reputation
Even in the cannon's mouth. And then the justice,[6]
In fair round belly with good capon[7] lined,
With eyes severe and beard of formal cut,
Full of wise saws and modern instances;[8]
And so he plays his part. The sixth age shifts

---

[1] players: actors
[2] ages: periods of life
[3] mewling (my$\overline{oo}$l´ ing): whimpering, crying like a baby
[4] pard (pärd): a leopard or panther
[5] Jealous in honor: very concerned about his honor
[6] justice: a judge
[7] capon (kā´ pän): a roasted chicken. The speaker is implying that the judge has been bribed with the present of a fat chicken.
[8] wise saws and modern instances: wise sayings and modern examples that show the truth of the sayings

Into the lean and slippered pantaloon,[9]
With spectacles on nose and pouch on side,
His youthful hose[10] well saved, a world too wide
For his shrunk shank;[11] and his big manly voice,
Turning again toward childish treble, pipes
And whistles in his sound. Last scene of all,
That ends this strange eventful history,
Is second childishness, and mere oblivion,
Sans[12] teeth, sans eyes, sans taste, sans everything.

WILLIAM SHAKESPEARE

---

[9] pantaloon (pan´ t'l $\overline{oo}$ n´): a thin, foolish old man—originally a
character in old comedies
[10] hose (hōz): stockings
[11] shank (shank): leg
[12] sans (sanz): without, lacking

# A SECRET FOR TWO

Quentin Reynolds

During the past fifteen years the horse which drew the milk wagon used by Pierre was a large white horse named Joseph. In Montreal, especially in that part of Montreal which is very French, the animals, like children, are often given the names of saints. When the big white horse first came to the Provinciale Milk Company he didn't have a name. They told Pierre that he could use the white horse henceforth. Pierre stroked the softness of the horse's neck; he stroked the sheen of its splendid belly and he looked into the eyes of the horse.

"This is a kind horse, a gentle and a faithful horse," Pierre said, "and I can see a beautiful spirit shining out of the eyes of the horse. I will name him after good St. Joseph, who was also kind and gentle and faithful and a beautiful spirit."

Within a year Joseph knew the milk route as well as Pierre. Pierre used to boast that he didn't need reins—he never touched them. Each morning Pierre arrived at the stables of the Provinciale Milk Company at five o'clock. The wagon would be loaded and Joseph hitched to it. Pierre would call, "*Bonjour, vieil ami,*" as he climbed into his seat and Joseph would turn his head and the other drivers would smile and say that the horse would smile at Pierre. Then Jacques, the foreman, would say, "All right, Pierre, go on," and Pierre would call softly to Joseph, "*Avance, mon ami,*" and this splendid combination would stalk proudly down the street.

The wagon, without any direction from Pierre, would roll three blocks down St. Catherine Street, then turn right two blocks along Roslyn Avenue; then left, for that was Prince Edward Street. The horse would stop at the first house, allow Pierre perhaps thirty seconds to get down from his seat and put a bottle of milk at the front door, and would then go on, skipping two houses and stopping at the third. So down the length of the street. Then Joseph, still without any direction from Pierre, would turn round and come back along the other side. Yes, Joseph was a smart horse.

Pierre would boast at the stable of Joseph's skill. "I never touch the reins. He knows just where to stop. Why, a blind man could handle my route with Joseph pulling the wagon."

So it went on for years—always the same. Pierre and Joseph both grew old together, but gradually, not suddenly. Pierre's huge walrus moustache was pure white now and Joseph didn't lift his knees so high or raise his head quite as much. Jacques, the foreman of the stables, never noticed that they were both getting old until Pierre appeared one morning carrying a heavy walking-stick.

"Hey, Pierre," Jacques laughed. "Maybe you got the gout, hey?"

"*Mais oui, Jacques,*" Pierre said a bit uncertainly. "One grows old. One's legs get tired."

"You should teach that horse to carry the milk to the front door for you," Jacques told him. "He does everything else."

He knew every one of the forty families he served on Prince Edward Street. The cooks knew that Pierre could neither read nor write; so instead of following the usual custom of leaving a note in an empty bottle if an additional quart of milk was needed, they would sing out when they heard the rumble of his wagon wheels over the cobbled street, "Bring an extra quart this morning, Pierre."

"So you have company for dinner tonight," he would call back gaily.

Pierre had a remarkable memory. When he arrived at the stable he'd always remember to tell Jacques, "The Paquins took an extra quart this morning; the Lemoines bought a pint of cream."

Jacques would note these things in a little book he always carried. Most of the drivers had to make out the weekly bills and collect the money, but Jacques, liking Pierre, had always excused him from this task. All Pierre had to do was to arrive at five in the morning, walk to his wagon, which was always in the same spot at the curb, and deliver his milk. He returned some two hours later, got down stiffly from his seat, called a cheery, "*Au'voir*" to Jacques and then limped slowly down the street.

One morning the president of the Provinciale Milk Company came to inspect the early morning deliveries. Jacques pointed Pierre out to him and said: "Watch how he talks to that horse. See how the horse listens and how he turns his head toward Pierre? See the look in that horse's eyes? You know I think those two share a secret. I have often noticed it. It is as though they both sometimes chuckle at us as they go off on their route. Pierre is a good man, *Monsieur Président*, but he gets old. Would it be too bold of me to suggest that he be retired and be given perhaps a small pension?" he added anxiously.

"But of course," the president laughed. "I know his record. He has been on this route now for thirty years and never once has there been a complaint. Tell him it is time he rested. His salary will go on just the same."

But Pierre refused to retire. He was panic-stricken at the thought of not driving Joseph every day. "We are two old men," he said to Jacques. "Let us wear out together. When Joseph is ready to retire—then I, too, will quit."

Jacques, who was a kind man, understood. There was something about Pierre and Joseph which made a man smile tenderly. It was as though each drew some hidden strength from the other. When Pierre was sitting in his seat, and when Joseph was hitched to the wagon, neither seemed old. But when they finished their work, then Pierre would limp down the street slowly, seeming very old indeed, and the horse's head would drop and he would walk very wearily to his stall.

Then one morning Jacques had dreadful news for Pierre when he arrived. It was a cold morning and still pitch-dark. The air was like iced wine that morning and the snow which had fallen during the night glistened like a million diamonds piled together.

Jacques said, "Pierre, your horse, Joseph, did not wake up this morning. He was very old, Pierre; he was twenty-five and that is like being seventy-five for a man."

"Yes," Pierre said, slowly. "Yes. I am seventy-five. And I cannot see Joseph again."

"Of course you can," Jacques soothed. "He is over in his stall, looking very peaceful. Go over and see him."

Pierre took one step forward then turned. "No . . . no . . . you don't understand, Jacques."

Jacques clapped him on the shoulder. "We'll find another horse just as good as Joseph. Why, in a month you'll teach him to know your route as well as Joseph did. We'll . . . "

The look in Pierre's eyes stopped him. For years, Pierre had worn a heavy cap, the peak of which came low over his eyes, keeping the bitter morning wind out of them. Now Jacques looked into Pierre's eyes and he saw something which startled him. He saw a dead, lifeless look in them. The eyes were mirroring the grief that was in Pierre's heart and his soul. It was as though his heart and soul had died.

"Take today off, Pierre," Jacques said, but already Pierre was hobbling off down the street, and had one been near, one would have seen tears streaming down his cheeks and have heard half-smothered sobs. There was a warning yell from the driver of a huge truck that was coming fast and there was the scream of brakes, but Pierre apparently heard neither.

Five minutes later an ambulance driver said, "He's dead. Was killed instantly."

"I couldn't help it," the driver of the truck protested, "he walked right into my truck. He never saw it, I guess. Why, he walked into it as though he were blind."

The ambulance doctor bent down, "Blind? Of course the man was blind. See those cataracts? This man has been blind for five years." He turned to Jacques, "You say he worked for you? Didn't you know he was blind?"

"No . . . no . . . " Jacques said, softly. "None of us knew. Only one knew—a friend of his named Joseph. . . . It was a secret, I think, just between those two."

# All the
# YEARS
## of her
# LIFE

Morley Callaghan

They were closing the drugstore, and Alfred Higgins, who had just taken off his white jacket, was putting on his coat and getting ready to go home. The little grey-haired man, Sam Carr, who owned the drugstore, was bending down behind the cash register, and when Alfred Higgins passed him, he looked up and said softly, "Just a moment, Alfred. One moment before you go."

The soft, confident, quiet way in which Sam Carr spoke made Alfred start to button his coat nervously. He felt sure his face was white. Sam Carr usually said, "Good night," brusquely, without looking up. In the six months he had been working in the drugstore Alfred had never heard his employer speak softly like that. His heart began to beat so loud it was hard for him to get his breath. "What is it, Mr. Carr?" he asked.

"Maybe you'd be good enough to take a few things out of your pocket and leave them here before you go," Sam Carr said.

"What things? What are you talking about?"

"You've got a compact and a lipstick and at least two tubes of toothpaste in your pockets, Alfred."

"What do you mean? Do you think I'm crazy?" Alfred blustered. His face got red and he knew he looked fierce with indignation. But Sam Carr, standing by the door with his blue eyes shining brightly behind his glasses and his lips moving underneath his grey moustache, only nodded his head a few times, and then Alfred grew very frightened and he didn't know what to say. Slowly he raised his hand and dipped it into his pocket, and with his eyes never meeting Sam Carr's eyes, he took out a blue compact and two tubes of toothpaste and a lipstick, and he laid them one by one on the counter.

"Petty thieving, eh, Alfred?" Sam Carr said. "And maybe you'd be good enough to tell me how long this has been going on."

"This is the first time I ever took anything."

"So now you think you'll tell me a lie, eh? What kind of a sap do I look like, huh? I don't know what goes on in my own store, eh? I tell you you've been doing this pretty steady." Sam Carr said as he went over and stood behind the cash register.

Ever since Alfred had left school he had been getting into trouble wherever he worked. He lived at home with his mother and his father, who was a printer. His two older brothers were married and his sister had got married last year, and it would have been all right for his parents now if Alfred had only been able to keep a job.

While Sam Carr smiled and stroked the side of his face very delicately with the tips of his fingers, Alfred began to feel that familiar terror growing in him that had been in him every time he had got into such trouble.

"I liked you," Sam Carr was saying. "I liked you and would have trusted you, and now look what I got to do." While Alfred watched with his alert, frightened blue eyes, Sam Carr drummed with his fingers on the counter. "I don't like to call a cop in point-blank," he was saying as he looked very worried. "You're a fool, and maybe I should call your father and tell him you're a fool. Maybe I should let him know I'm going to have you locked up."

"My father's not at home. He's a printer. He works nights," Alfred said.

"Who's at home?"

"My mother, I guess."

"Then we'll see what she says." Sam Carr went to the phone and dialed the number. Alfred was not so much ashamed, but there was that deep fright growing in him, and he blurted out arrogantly, like a strong, full-grown man, "Just a minute. You don't need to draw anybody else in. You don't need to tell her." He wanted to sound like a swaggering, big guy who could look after himself, yet the old, childish hope was in him, the longing that someone at home would come and help him. "Yeah, that's right, he's in trouble." Mr. Carr was saying. "Yeah, your boy works for me. You'd better come down in a hurry." And when he was finished Mr. Carr went over to the door and looked out at the street and watched the people passing in the late summer night. "I'll keep my eye out for a cop," was all he said.

Alfred knew how his mother would come rushing in; she would rush in with her eyes blazing, or maybe she would be crying, and she would push him away when he tried to talk to her, and make him feel her dreadful con- tempt; yet he longed that she might come before Mr. Carr saw the cop on the beat passing the door.

While they waited—and it seemed a long time—they

did not speak, and when at last they heard someone tapping on the closed door, Mr. Carr, turning the latch, said crisply, "Come in, Mrs. Higgins." He looked hard-faced and stern.

Mrs. Higgins must have been going to bed when he telephoned, for her hair was tucked in loosely under her hat, and her hand at her throat held her light coat tight across her chest so her dress would not show. She came in, large and plump, with a little smile on her friendly face. Most of the store lights had been turned out and at first she did not see Alfred, who was standing in the shadow at the end of the counter. Yet as soon as she saw him she did not look as Alfred thought she would look: she smiled, her blue eyes never wavered, and with a calmness and dignity that made them forget that her clothes seemed to have been thrown on her, she put out her hand to Mr. Carr and said politely, "I'm Mrs. Higgins. I'm Alfred's mother."

Mr. Carr was a bit embarrassed by her lack of terror and her simplicity, and he hardly knew what to say to her, so she asked, "Is Alfred in trouble?"

"He is. He's been taking things from the store. I caught him red-handed. Little things like compacts and toothpaste and lipsticks. "Stuff he can sell easily," the proprietor said.

As she listened Mrs. Higgins looked at Alfred sometimes and nodded her head sadly, and when Sam Carr had finished she said gravely, "Is it so, Alfred?"

"Yes."

"Why have you been doing it?"

"I been spending money, I guess."

"On what?"

"Going around with the guys, I guess," Alfred said.

Mrs. Higgins put out her hand and touched Sam

Carr's arm with an understanding gentleness, and speaking as though afraid of disturbing him, she said, "If you would only listen to me before doing anything." Her simple earnestness made her shy; her humility made her falter and look away, but in a moment she was smiling gravely again, and she said with a kind of patient dignity, "What did you intend to do, Mr. Carr?"

"I was going to get a cop. That's what I ought to do."

"Yes, I suppose so. It's not for me to say, because he's my son. Yet I sometimes think a little good advice is the best thing for a boy when he's at a certain period in his life," she said.

Alfred couldn't understand his mother's quiet composure, for if they had been at home and someone had suggested that he was going to be arrested, he knew she would be in a rage and would cry out against him. Yet now she was standing there with that gentle, pleading smile on her face, saying, "I wonder if you don't think it would be better just to let him come home with me. He looks a big fellow, doesn't he? It takes some of them a long time to get any sense," and they both stared at Alfred, who shifted away with a bit of light shining for a moment on his thin face and the tiny pimples over his cheekbone.

But even while he was turning away uneasily Alfred was realizing that Mr. Carr had become aware that his mother was really a fine woman; he knew that Sam Carr was puzzled by his mother, as if he had expected her to come in and plead with him tearfully, and instead he was being made to feel a bit ashamed by her vast tolerance. While there was only the sound of the mother's soft, assured voice in the store, Mr. Carr began to nod his head encouragingly at her. Without being alarmed, while being just large and still and simple and hopeful, she was becoming dominant there in the dimly lit store. "Of course, I don't want to be harsh," Mr. Carr was saying. "I'll tell you what I'll do. I'll just fire him and let it go at that. How's that?" and he got up and shook hands with Mrs. Higgins, bowing low to her in deep respect.

There was such warmth and gratitude in the way she said, "I'll never forget your kindness," that Mr. Carr began to feel warm and genial himself.

"Sorry we had to meet this way," he said. "But I'm glad I got in touch with you. Just wanted to do the right thing, that's all," he said.

"It's better to meet like this than never, isn't it?" she said. Suddenly they clasped hands as if they liked each other, as if they had known each other a long time. "Good night, sir." she said.

"Good night, Mrs. Higgins. I'm truly sorry," he said.

The mother and son walked along the street together, and the mother was taking a long, firm stride as she looked ahead with her stern face full of worry. Alfred was afraid to speak to her, he was afraid of the silence that was between them, so he only looked ahead too, for the excitement and relief was still pretty strong in him; but in a little while, going along like that in silence made him terribly aware of the strength and the sternness in her; he began to wonder what she was thinking of as she stared ahead so grimly; she seemed to have forgotten that he walked beside her; so when they were passing under the railway bridge and the rumble of the train seemed to break the silence, he said in his old, bluster-way, "Thank goodness it turned out like that. I certainly won't get in a jam like that again."

"Be quiet. Don't speak to me. You've disgraced me again and again," she said bitterly.

"That's the last time. That's all I'm saying."

"Have the decency to be quiet," she snapped. They kept on their way, looking straight ahead.

When they were at home and his mother took off her coat, Alfred saw that she was really only half-dressed, and she made him feel afraid again when she said, without even looking at him, "You're a bad lot. God forgive you. It's one thing after another and always has been. Why do you stand there stupidly? Go to bed, why don't you?" When he was going, she said, "I'm going to make myself a cup of tea. Mind, now, not a word about tonight to your father."

While Alfred was undressing in his bedroom, he heard his mother moving around the kitchen. She filled the kettle and put it on the stove. She moved a chair. And as he listened there was no shame in him, just wonder and a kind of admiration of her strength and repose. He could still see Sam Carr nodding his head encouragingly to her; he could hear her talking simply and earnestly, and as he sat on his bed he felt a pride in her strength. "She certainly was smooth," he thought. "Gee, I'd like to tell her she sounded swell."

And at last he got up and went along to the kitchen, and when he was at the door he saw his mother pouring herself a cup of tea. He watched and he didn't move. Her face, as she sat there, was a frightened, broken face utterly unlike the face of the woman who had been so assured a little while ago in the drugstore. When she reached out and lifted the kettle to pour hot water in her cup, her hand trembled and the water splashed on the stove. Leaning back in the chair, she sighed and lifted the cup to her lips, and her lips were groping loosely as if they would never reach the cup. She swallowed the hot tea eagerly, and then she straightened up in relief, though her hand holding the cup still trembled. She looked very old.

It seemed to Alfred that this was the way it had been every time he had been in trouble before, that this trembling had really been in her as she hurried out half-dressed to the drugstore. He understood why she had sat alone in the kitchen the night his young sister had kept repeating doggedly that she was getting married. Now he felt all that his mother had been thinking of as they walked along the street together a little while ago. He watched his mother, and he never spoke, but at that moment his youth seemed to be over; he knew all the years of her life by the way her hand trembled as she raised the cup to her lips. It seemed to him that this was the first time he had ever looked upon his mother.

# Thank You, Ma'am

Langston Hughes

She was a large woman with a large purse that had everything in it but a hammer and nails. It had a long strap, and she carried it slung across her shoulder. It was about eleven o'clock at night, dark, and she was walking alone, when a boy ran up behind her and tried to snatch her purse. The strap broke with the sudden single tug the boy gave it from behind. But the boy's weight and the weight of the purse combined caused him to lose his balance. Instead of taking off full blast as he had hoped, the boy fell on his back on the sidewalk and his legs flew up. The large woman simply turned around and kicked him right square in his blue-jeaned sitter. Then she reached down, picked the boy up by his shirt front, and shook him until his teeth rattled.

After that the woman said, "Pick up my pocketbook, boy, and give it here."

She still held him tightly. But she bent down enough

to permit him to stoop and pick up her purse. Then she said, "Now ain't you ashamed of yourself?"

Firmly gripped by his shirt front, the boy said, "Yes'm."

The woman said, "What did you want to do it for?"

The boy said, "I didn't aim to."

She said, "You a lie!"

By that time two or three people passed, stopped, turned to look, and some stood watching.

"If I turn you loose, will you run?" asked the woman.

"Yes'm," said the boy.

"Then I won't turn you loose," said the woman. She did not release him.

"Lady, I'm sorry," whispered the boy.

"Um-hum! Your face is dirty. I got a great mind to wash your face for you. Ain't you got nobody home to tell you to wash your face?"

"No'm," said the boy.

"Then it will get washed this evening," said the large woman, starting up the street, dragging the frightened boy behind her.

He looked as if he were fourteen or fifteen, frail and willow-wild, in tennis shoes and blue jeans.

The woman said, "You ought to be my son. I would teach you right from wrong. Least I can do right now is to wash your face. Are you hungry?"

"No'm," said the being-dragged boy. "I just want you to turn me loose."

"Was I bothering *you* when I turned that corner?" asked the woman.

"No'm."

"But you put yourself in contact with *me*," said the woman. "If you think that that contact is not going to last awhile, you got another thought coming. When I get through with you, sir, you are going to remember Mrs. Luella Bates Washington Jones."

Sweat popped out on the boy's face and he began to struggle. Mrs. Jones stopped, jerked him around in front of her, put a half nelson about his neck, and continued to drag him up the street. When she got to her door, she dragged the boy inside, down a hall, and into a large kitchenette-furnished room at the rear of the house. She switched on the light and left the door open. The boy could hear other roomers laughing and talking in the large house. Some of their doors were open, too, so he knew he and the woman were not alone. The woman still had him by the neck in the middle of her room.

She said, "What is your name?"

"Roger," answered the boy.

"Then, Roger, you go to that sink and wash your face," said the woman, whereupon she turned him loose—at last. Roger looked at the door—looked at the woman—looked at the door—*and went to the sink*.

"Let the water run until it gets warm," she said. "Here's a clean towel."

"You gonna take me to jail?" asked the boy, bending over the sink.

"Not with that face, I would not take you nowhere," said the woman. "Here I am trying to get home to cook me a bite to eat, and you snatch my pocketbook! Maybe you ain't been to your supper either, late as it be. Have you?"

"There's nobody home at my house," said the boy.

"Then we'll eat," said the woman. "I believe you're hungry—or been hungry—to try to snatch my pocket-book!"

"I want a pair of blue suede shoes," said the boy.

"Well, you didn't have to snatch *my* pocketbook to

get some suede shoes," said Mrs. Luella Bates Washington Jones. "You could of asked me."

"Ma'am?"

The water dripping from his face, the boy looked at her. There was a long pause. A very long pause. After he had dried his face and not knowing what else to do, dried it again, the boy turned around, wondering what next. The door was open. He could make a dash for it down the hall. He could run, run, run, *run!*

The woman was sitting on the day bed. After a while she said, "I were young once and I wanted things I could not get."

There was another long pause. The boy's mouth opened. Then he frowned, not knowing he frowned.

The woman said, "Um-hum! You thought I was going to say *but,* didn't you? You thought I was going to say, *but I didn't snatch people's pocketbooks.* Well, I wasn't going to say that." Pause. Silence. "I have done things, too, which I would not tell you, son—neither tell God, if He didn't already know. Everybody's got something in common. So you set down while I fix us something to eat. You might run that comb through your hair so you will look presentable."

In another corner of the room behind a screen was a gas plate and an icebox. Mrs. Jones got up and went behind the screen. The woman did not watch the boy to see if he was going to run now, nor did she watch her purse, which she left behind her on the day bed. But the boy took care to sit on the far side of the room, away from the purse, where he thought she could easily see him out of the corner of her eye if she wanted to. He did not trust the woman *not* to trust him. And he did not want to be mistrusted now.

"Do you need somebody to go to the store," asked

the boy, "maybe to get some milk or something?"

"Don't believe I do," said the woman, "unless you just want sweet milk yourself. I was going to make cocoa out of this canned milk I got here."

"That will be fine," said the boy.

She heated some lima beans and ham she had in the icebox, made the cocoa, and set the table. The woman did not ask the boy anything about where he lived, or his folks, or anything else that would embarrass him. Instead, as they ate, she told him about her job in a hotel beauty shop that stayed open late, what the work was like, and how all kinds of women came in and out, blondes, redheads, and Spanish. Then she cut him a half of her ten-cent cake.

"Eat some more, son," she said.

When they were finished eating, she got up and said, "Now here, take this ten dollars and buy yourself some blue suede shoes. And next time, do not make the mistake of latching onto *my* pocketbook *nor nobody else's*— because shoes got by devilish ways will burn your feet. I got to get my rest now. But from here on in, son, I hope you will behave yourself."

She led him down the hall to the front door and opened it. "Good night! Behave yourself, boy!" she said, looking out into the street as he went down the steps.

The boy wanted to say something other than, "Thank you, ma'am," to Mrs. Luella Bates Washington Jones, but although his lips moved, he couldn't even say that as he turned at the foot of the barren stoop and looked up at the large woman in the door. Then she shut the door.

## Looking Out

It must be odd
to be a minority
he was saying.
I looked around
and didn't see any.
So I said
Yeah
it must be.

MITSUYE YAMADA

## Now

People ask me all the time
what will you be
when you grow up?

I tell them I'll be
a computer programmer
or maybe a doctor
or maybe work in a bank
like my aunt
but what I want to say
is
what's wrong with me now?

MAVIS JONES

# THE DAY THE WAR CAME TO HALIFAX

Julian Beltrame

*In 1917, during World War I, a disaster occurred in the harbor of Halifax, Nova Scotia. When a French ship carrying highly sensitive explosives collided with a Norwegian ship, the resulting blast rocked the world.*

Halifax—the doomed ships steamed unwaveringly toward collision, like two trains on the same narrow track.

Or so it seemed to Barbara Orr, gazing out her front window at the morning traffic in the harbor below.

For the six Orr children, Dec. 6, 1917, was a red-letter day. One had come down with measles, so all were excused from school. The view from the front window was unimpeded and, on this fateful morning, a fiery sun painted the harbor in shimmering gold. Barbara could count ships all day.

But there was something odd about these two ships.

One, moving slowly from Barbara's right toward the Bedford basin, at the far end of the channel, hugged the Dartmouth coast as if crowded out of the channel by bigger ships.

The second, a larger, swifter vessel with the large red letters BELGIAN RELIEF on its white side, was obviously coming from the basin and heading to Halifax harbor proper, and then to open sea. Strangely, it was cutting across the centre of the channel, making straight for the other ship.

From about two kilometres away, it did not seem so much a collision as a love peck. But within seconds, Barbara could see a spiralling ribbon of black smoke rising from the front of the smaller ship and she knew it must have been quite a smack.

"They looked as if they were deliberately trying to run into each other," the 13-year-old excitedly told her mother, Annie.

It didn't take much convincing for Barbara and two younger brothers to hound Annie into letting them go down to the shore to watch the fire. A lot of people in Halifax's working-class north end had a similar notion.

It was shortly after 8:30 a.m. and the sight of the ship, now burning out of control and drifting toward the shore, drew many curious onlookers, including her father, Samuel.

Barbara was so excited about what the morning would offer—fire, men scrambling to put it out, the ships that were gravitating toward the emergency—that she just had to share it with her friend.

"I'll come down in a few minutes," she told her brother.

Barbara does not remember whether she had time to find her friend. She remembers a loud roar, somersaulting in the air, and landing with a jolt more than 30 metres away. She was covered with oil and soot; her face stung with cuts. She felt a searing pain in her foot and saw her tightly laced boot was gone.

Barbara's first thought was for her home, but she could not move. Her foot, which had been crushed by her tumble, ached with pain.

Slowly, she crawled a few metres so she could see where her home had been, but she saw only a black wall of smoke.

She cried out for help, but everyone was scurrying about, paying no attention to her. It took her an unbearably long time to crawl to her aunt's home on Gottingen Street.

Barbara doesn't remember when she was taken to Camp Hill hospital. She remembers being loaded on to the Boutilier fishwagon, used to pick up the wounded. Then everything was fine again.

When Robert Oppenheimer, head of the U.S. Manhattan Project that created the atomic bomb, wanted to visualize what destructive powers would be unleashed by his new weapon, he studied the devastation of the Halifax explosion.

No better model existed. The explosion was the single greatest man-made detonation in history, not bettered until Oppenheimer's own invention was dropped on Hiroshima.

The destruction, while confined to a smaller area and without the curse of radiation, was similar to Hiroshima.

In all, between 2 000 and 3 000 people perished, some vanished into thin air so that their deaths, their identities and even the knowledge of their existence remains a mystery today. More than 10 000 were injured,

3 000 horribly enough to require extensive hospitalization. About 200 were blinded.

The tragedy would forever change Halifax's topography. More than 12 000 buildings within a 25-kilometre radius were seriously damaged, 1 600 destroyed.

It really did seem, as Barbara Orr told her mother, as if the two ships set out to collide or as if fate had decreed Canada would not be spared direct knowledge of the savagery of the European conflict.

A series of coincidences, human error and unfathomable decisions from previously capable and experienced sailors converged in one place and time. The sum of these parts was destruction of a kind few would have guessed possible.

It was unexpected that Capt. Aime Le Medec, the 38-year-old commander of the French freighter Mont Blanc, should find himself at the mouth of Halifax harbor on the morning of Dec. 6, 1917.

He had been set to sail for France from New York in late November. But his munitions ship, really a glorified tug on its last sea legs, could muster at most eight knots and, hence, would have represented a danger to the small convoy setting out from New York.

The convoy would be travelling at about 13 knots, Le Medec was told, but he might be able to hitch on to an escort that would protect the Mont Blanc from marauding German U-boats if he were to join a larger convoy, amassing in Halifax.

The Mont Blanc was singularly in need of protection. Carrying 2 300 tonnes of picric acid—a sensitive explosive agent more destructive than TNT—200 tonnes of TNT, 35 tonnes of benzole, and 10 tonnes of gun cotton, it made an alluring target.

And so it was that Le Medec found himself awaiting permission to enter the harbor as a bright sun rose on the starboard side.

What put Norwegian Capt. Haakon From in the harbor that morning was a bit of hard luck. He had been promised 50 tonnes of steam fuel for the Imo's voyage to New York by 3 p.m. the day before. But it was 5:30 p.m. when the fuel arrived, dusk had descended and the harbor was closed for the day.

Fate had set the table, now it was up to man's stupidity, pride, short-sightedness and just plain pig-headedness to play their parts.

At 7:37 a.m., Le Medec was cleared to enter the harbor, telling an inquiring officer it was not necessary to hoist a red flag, signalling the sensitive nature of the ship's cargo. The order was well within regulations, for a red flag would alert the Germans as well as warn friendly ships.

Still piqued over the unnecessary delay, From did not wait for permission to set off and steamed out of Bedford basin. The Imo was making as much as seven knots when it entered the Narrows, an 800-metre channel connecting the basin with the harbor proper, like the neck of an hourglass.

Le Medec, following harbor procedures, kept the Mont Blanc to the Dartmouth side of the channel when, to his amazement, he spotted the approaching Imo headed straight toward him.

He whistled a sharp blast of warning, and headed closer to shore, to within 300 metres from shore, when the reply came from the Imo. Two blasts, indicating From was altering course putting him even more across Mont Blanc's bow.

Cursing, Le Medec stopped his engines and repeated

the single blast signal. Again came Imo's reply, two blasts and full speed ahead.

Suddenly, Le Medec realized there was only one thing left to do, bear left to port. This time the puzzling Imo signalled three blasts, meaning she was reversing her engines. This had the effect of swinging her head starboard and onto the Mont Blanc, ripping into the munition ship's No. 1 hold.

Later, judicial hearings would determine that both captains could have avoided the collision by recognizing the danger earlier and reversing their course. But once the sequence of actions was initiated, there seemed to be no turning back.

The time it took for the sparks from scraping metal to ignite the benzole, flowing freely on the main deck and onto the unstable lyddite on the ruptured No. 1 hold, could be measured in seconds.

Nor did the horrified Mont Blanc captain take long to measure his response.

"Abandon ship!" he yelled. It was about 8:45 a.m. With the speed of men who knew only distance could save them from certain death, they jumped for the two lifeboats and literally headed for the hills on the Dartmouth shore.

The Mont Blanc, now burning freely, drifted toward and then struck Pier 6 on the Halifax shore, attracting a swarm of spectators, emergency personnel, and other ships in the harbor.

They drew in close for a better look at the unfolding drama, or they may have genuinely wanted to help fight the fire. With no red flag showing, they were tragically unaware of the catastrophe now minutes away.

Lt.-Cmdr James Murray was one of only a handful aware of the danger. As sea transport officer, he had been notified of the Mont Blanc that week and now he was on the deck of the Hilford, not more than a few hundred metres from the burning freighter.

No one knows what Murray thought, for he would not survive the half-hour, but what he did is well known. He was about to become the first of many heroes of the day.

He set the Hilford for Pier 9, where he could send out a general warning from his office, but would place him perilously close to the explosion. And he ordered a sailor to the railway yards.

The first reactions of dispatcher Vince Coleman and chief clerk Bill Lovett, upon hearing the panicked sailor's dire warning, were to run like heck. But Coleman remembered two trains were due soon from Rockingham and Truro.

"Bill, I know (the danger) but someone's got to stop those trains," Lovett recalled the second hero of the pending disaster saying before Coleman returned to tap out the last message he would ever send.

In the blink of an eye, the Mont Blanc disappeared into a ball of fire. The force of the explosion propelled its half-tonne anchor shaft to the Northwest Arm three kilometres away, and its forward gun barrel melted away into Albro's Lake, almost two kilometres behind Dartmouth.

The scenes of destruction have been told in hundreds of testimonials, diaries, letters and news articles.

Some talk about headless bodies, or of a severed arm protruding from rubble of wood and brick. Diaries talk of dead bodies lying on the road. Emergency crews cite incidents of having to abandon whole families, burning alive under collapsed homes, because attempting a futile rescue meant ignoring more hopeful cases.

The blast was so great that practically every window in the city was exploded into a windstorm of glass shards, blinding some, tattooing other survivors with specs of blue still visible today. Survivors talk about an earthquake and a tidal wave that drenched them hundreds of metres inland.

As total as the devastation appeared to be from photographs of the period, it also exhibited a fickle side.

One survivor, Millicent Swindells, now 78, was asleep in her upstairs bedroom when the Mont Blanc blew up. She heard no noise.

"All I know was one moment I was in bed, the next I was standing in the hall," she says.

Her father was also in bed, which overturned on top of him. He emerged with a scratch on his foot. A brother had his back to a window and was peppered with tiny glass cuts.

Her mother and four siblings were in the east side of the house. It was obliterated. They all died.

"I remember going out and one of the kids said, 'Oh, Millie, your eye is out on your cheek.' It had been sucked out by the air concussion and I wasn't aware of it." Millicent later lost the eye.

And there were stories of wondrous miracles, like that of the young unidentified woman on Campbell Road who had been thrown to the street by the blast. A soldier offered her his coat and when she looked down, she saw she was wearing only her corsets. The concussion had sucked away her coat and dress, even her stockings and shoes, but otherwise left her completely untouched.

And there were the stories historians can only guess at.

"I still get calls asking me to help with identities," says Janet Kitz, who has worked on identifying remains of the dead for the Maritime Museum of the Atlantic.

"One woman called because she heard a rumor her two children, whom she never found, were seen on a ship. Seventy years later, she still cannot reconcile herself that they were lost."

Few lost as much that day as Barbara Orr.

Her father, Samuel, was on his way to work at the paintworks that morning. He never made it. Her mother and the three youngest children were swallowed up by their collapsing home. The other two brothers, watching firefighters trying to put out the flames, were killed when the ship exploded.

In 1920, Barbara presented the Kaye-Grove Church with a magnificent chime of bells in memory of her lost family.

For close to 50 years the bells rang at the church, until the failing tower could no longer hold them.

On June 9, 1985, the 10 bronze bells made their appearance again. With hundreds looking on, Barbara again played the carillon. But this time it was on the crown of Fort Needham, where they had been installed in a new tower that today stands as the only monument to the day the war came to Halifax.

# (Nothing But) FLOWERS

Here we stand
Like an Adam and an Eve
Waterfalls
    The Garden of Eden
    *Two fools in love*
So beautiful and strong
The birds in the trees
Are smiling upon them
From the age of the dinosaurs
Cars have run on gasoline
Where, where have they gone?
Now, it's nothing but flowers
There was a factory
Now there are mountains and rivers
You got it, you got it
We caught a rattlesnake
Now we got something for dinner
We got it, we got it
There was a shopping mall
Now it's all covered with flowers
You've got it, you've got it
If this is paradise
I wish I had a lawnmower
You've got it, we've got it

Years ago
I was an angry young man
I'd pretend
That I was a billboard
Standing tall
By the side of the road
I fell in love
With a beautiful highway

This used to be real estate
Now it's only fields and trees
Where, where is the town
Now, it's nothing but flowers
The highways and cars
Were sacrificed for agriculture
I thought that we'd start over
But I guess I was wrong

Once there were parking lots
Now it's a peaceful oasis
    YOU GOT IT, YOU GOT IT
This was a Pizza Hut
Now it's all covered with daisies
    YOU GOT IT, YOU GOT IT
I miss the honky tonks,
Dairy Queens and 7-Elevens
YOU GOT IT, YOU GOT IT
And as things fell apart
Nobody paid much attention
    YOU GOT IT, YOU GOT IT

I dream of cherry pies,
Candy bars and chocolate chip cookies
    YOU GOT IT, YOU GOT IT
We used to microwave,
Now we just eat nuts and berries
    YOU GOT IT, YOU GOT IT
This was a discount store,
Now it's turned into a cornfield
YOU GOT IT, YOU GOT IT
Don't leave me stranded here,
I can't get used to this lifestyle

DAVID BYRNE

# Buffalo Dusk

The buffaloes are gone.
And those who saw the buffaloes are gone.
Those who saw the buffaloes by thousands and how they
    pawed the prairie sod into dust with their great hoofs,
    their great heads down pawing on in a great pageant
    of dusk,
Those who saw the buffaloes are gone.
And the buffaloes are gone.

CARL   SANDBURG

# Drums of My Father

A hundred thousand years have passed
Yet, I hear the distant beat of my father's drums
I hear his drums throughout the land
His beat I feel within my heart.

The drums shall beat, so my heart shall beat,
And I shall live a hundred thousand years.

SHIRLEY   DANIELS

# THE
# All-American
# SLURP

Lensey Namioka

The first time our family was invited out to dinner in America, we disgraced ourselves while eating celery. We had emigrated to this country from China, and during our early days here we had a hard time with American table manners.

In China we never ate celery raw, or any other kind of vegetable raw. We always had to disinfect the vegetables in boiling water first. When we were presented with our first relish tray, the raw celery caught us unprepared.

We had been invited to dinner by our neighbors, the Gleasons. After arriving at the house, we shook hands with our hosts and packed ourselves into a sofa. As our family of four sat stiffly in a row, my youngest brother and I stole glances at our parents for a clue as to what to do next.

Mrs. Gleason offered the relish tray to Mother. The tray looked pretty, with its tiny red radishes, curly sticks of carrots, and long, slender stalks of pale green celery. "Do try some of the celery, Mrs. Lin," she said. "It's from a local farmer, and it's sweet."

Mother picked up one of the green stalks, and Father followed suit. Then I picked up a stalk, and my brother did too. So there we sat, each with a stalk of celery in our right hand.

Mrs. Gleason kept smiling. "Would you like to try some of the dip, Mrs. Lin? It's my own recipe: sour cream and onion flakes, with a dash of Tabasco sauce."

Most Chinese don't care for dairy products, and in those days I wasn't even ready to drink fresh milk. Sour cream sounded perfectly revolting. Our family shook our heads in unison.

Mrs. Gleason went off with the relish tray to the other guests, and we carefully watched to see what they did. Everyone seemed to eat the raw vegetables quite happily.

Mother took a bite of her celery. *Crunch.* "It's not bad!" she whispered.

Father took a bite of his celery. *Crunch.* "Yes, it *is* good," he said, looking surprised.

I took a bite, and then my brother. *Crunch, crunch.* It was more than good; it was delicious. Raw celery has a slight sparkle, a zingy taste that you don't get in cooked celery. When Mrs. Gleason came around with the relish tray, we each took another stalk of celery, except my brother. He took two.

There was only one problem: long strings ran through the length of the stalk, and they got caught in my teeth. When I help my mother in the kitchen, I always pull the strings out before slicing celery.

I pulled the strings out of my stalk. *Z-z-zip, z-z-zip.* My brother followed suit. *Z-z-zip, z-z-zip, z-z-zip.* To my left, my parents were taking care of their own stalks. *Z-z-zip, z-z-zip, z-z-zip.*

Suddenly I realized that there was dead silence except for our zipping. Looking up, I saw that the eyes of everyone in the room were on our family. Mr. and Mrs. Gleason, their daughter Meg, who was my friend, and their neighbors the Badels—they were all staring at us as we busily pulled the strings of our celery.

That wasn't the end of it. Mrs. Gleason announced that dinner was served and invited us to the dining table. It was lavishly covered with platters of food, but we couldn't see any chairs around the table. So we helpfully carried over some dining chairs and sat down. All the other guests just stood there.

Mrs. Gleason bent down and whispered to us, "This is a buffet dinner. You help yourselves to some food and eat it in the living room."

Our family beat a retreat back to the sofa as if chased by enemy soldiers. For the rest of the evening, too mortified to go back to the dining table, I nursed a bit of potato salad on my plate.

Next day Meg and I got on the school bus together. I wasn't sure how she would feel about me after the spectacle our family made at the party. But she was just the same as usual, and the only reference she made to the party was, "Hope you and your folks got enough to eat last night. You certainly didn't take very much. Mom never tries to figure out how much food to prepare. She just puts everything on the table and hopes for the best."

I began to relax. The Gleasons' dinner party wasn't so different from a Chinese meal after all. My mother also puts everything on the table and hopes for the best.

Meg was the first friend I had made after we came to America. I eventually got acquainted with a few other kids in school, but Meg was still the only real friend I had.

My brother didn't have any problems making friends. He spent all his time with some boys who were teaching him baseball, and in no time he could speak English much faster than I could—not better, but faster.

I worried more about making mistakes, and I spoke carefully, making sure I could say everything right before opening my mouth. At least I had a better accent than my parents, who never really got rid of their Chinese accent, even years later. My parents had both studied English in school before coming to America, but what they had studied was mostly written English, not spoken.

Father's approach to English was a scientific one. Since Chinese verbs have no tense, he was fascinated by the way English verbs changed form according to whether they were in the present, past imperfect, perfect, pluperfect, future, or future perfect tense. He was always making diagrams of verbs and their inflections, and he looked for opportunities to show off his mastery of the pluperfect and future perfect tenses, his two favorites. "I shall have finished my project by Monday," he would say smugly.

Mother's approach was to memorize lists of polite phrases that would cover all possible social situations. She was constantly muttering things like "I'm fine, thank you. And you?" Once she accidentally stepped on someone's foot, and hurriedly blurted, "Oh, that's quite all right!" Embarrassed by her slip, she resolved to do better next time. So when someone stepped on *her* foot, she cried, "You're welcome!"

In our different ways, we made progress in learning

English. But I had another worry, and that was my appearance. My brother didn't have to worry, since Mother bought him blue jeans for school, and he dressed like all the other boys. But she insisted that girls had to wear skirts. By the time she saw that Meg and the other girls were wearing jeans, it was too late. My school clothes were bought already, and we didn't have money left to buy new outfits for me. We had too many other things to buy first, like furniture, pots, and pans.

The first time I visited Meg's house, she took me upstairs to her room, and I wound up trying on her clothes. We were pretty much the same size, since Meg was shorter and thinner than average. Maybe that's how we became friends in the first place. Wearing Meg's jeans and T-shirt, I looked at myself in the mirror. I could almost pass for an American—from the back, anyway. At least the kids in school wouldn't stop and stare at me in the hallways, which was what they did when they saw me in my white blouse and navy blue skirt that went a couple of inches below the knees.

When Meg came to my house, I invited her to try on my Chinese dresses, the ones with a high collar and slits up the sides. Meg's eyes were bright as she looked at herself in the mirror. She struck several sultry poses, and we nearly fell over laughing.

The dinner party at the Gleasons' didn't stop my growing friendship with Meg. Things were getting better for me in other ways too. Mother finally bought me some jeans at the end of the month, when Father got his paycheck. She wasn't in any hurry about buying them at first, until I worked on her. This is what I did. Since we didn't have a car in those days, I often ran down to the neighborhood store to pick up things for her. The groceries cost less at a big supermarket, but the closest one was many blocks away. One day, when she ran out of flour, I offered to borrow a bike from our neighbor's son and buy a ten-pound bag of flour at the big supermarket. I mounted the boy's bike and waved to Mother. "I'll be back in five minutes!"

Before I started pedaling, I heard her voice behind me. "You can't go out in public like that! People can see all the way up to your thighs!"

"I'm sorry," I said innocently. "I thought you were in a hurry to get the flour." For dinner we were going to have pot-stickers (fried Chinese dumplings), and we needed a lot of flour.

"Couldn't you borrow a girl's bicycle?" complained Mother. "That way your skirt won't be pushed up."

"There aren't too many of those around," I said. "Almost all the girls wear jeans while riding a bike, so they don't see any point buying a girl's bike."

We didn't eat pot-stickers that evening, and Mother was thoughtful. Next day we took the bus downtown and she bought me a pair of jeans. In the same week, my brother made the baseball team of his junior high school, Father started taking driving lessons, and Mother discovered rummage sales. We soon got all the furniture we needed, plus a dart board and a 1,000-piece jigsaw puzzle (fourteen hours later, we discovered that it was a 999-piece jigsaw puzzle). There was hope that the Lins might become a normal American family after all.

Then came our dinner at the Lakeview restaurant.

The Lakeview was an expensive restaurant, one of those places where a headwaiter dressed in tails conducted you to your seat, and the only light came from candles and flaming desserts. In one corner of the room a lady harpist played tinkling melodies.

Father wanted to celebrate, because he had just been promoted. He worked for an electronics company, and after his English started improving, his superiors decided to appoint him to a position more suited to his training. The promotion not only brought a higher salary but was also a tremendous boost to his pride.

Up to then we had eaten only in Chinese restaurants. Although my brother and I were becoming fond of hamburgers, my parents didn't care much for western food, other than chow mein.

But this was a special occasion, and Father asked his coworkers to recommend a really elegant restaurant. So there we were at the Lakeview, stumbling after the headwaiter in the murky dining room.

At our table we were handed our menus, and they were so big that to read mine I almost had to stand up again. But why bother? It was mostly in French, anyway.

Father, being an engineer, was always systematic. He took out a pocket French dictionary. "They told me that most of the items would be in French, so I came prepared." He even had a pocket flashlight, the size of a marking pen. While Mother held the flashlight over the menu, he looked up the items that were in French.

"*Pâté en croûte*," he muttered. "Let's see . . . *pâté* is paste . . . *croûte* is crust . . . hmm . . . a paste in crust."

The waiter stood looking patient. I squirmed and died at least fifty times.

At long last Father gave up. "Why don't we just order four complete dinners at random?" he suggested.

"Isn't that risky?" asked Mother. "The French eat some rather peculiar things, I've heard."

"A Chinese can eat anything a Frenchman can eat," Father declared.

The soup arrived in a plate. How do you get soup up from a plate? I glanced at the other diners, but the ones at the nearby tables were not on their soup course, while the more distant ones were invisible in the darkness.

Fortunately my parents had studied books on western etiquette before they came to America. "Tilt your plate," whispered my mother. "It's easier to spoon the soup up that way."

She was right. Tilting the plate did the trick. But the etiquette book didn't say anything about what you did after the soup reached your lips. As any respectable Chinese knows, the correct way to eat your soup is to slurp. This helps to cool the liquid and prevent you from burning your lips. It also shows your appreciation.

We showed our appreciation. *Shloop*, went my father. *Shloop*, went my mother. *Shloop, shloop*, went my brother, who was the hungriest.

The lady harpist stopped playing to take a rest. And in the silence, our family's consumption of soup suddenly seemed unnaturally loud. You know how it sounds on a rocky beach when the tide goes out and the water drains from all those little pools? They go *shloop, shloop, shloop*. That was the Lin family, eating soup.

At the next table a waiter was pouring wine. When a large *shloop* reached him, he froze. The bottle continued to pour, and red wine flooded the tabletop and into the lap of a customer. Even the customer didn't notice anything at first, being also hypnotized by the *shloop, shloop, shloop*.

It was too much. "I need to go to the toilet," I mumbled, jumping to my feet. A waiter, sensing my urgency, quickly directed me to the ladies' room.

I splashed cold water on my burning face, and as I dried myself with a paper towel, I stared into the mirror.

In this perfumed ladies' room, with its pink-and-silver wallpaper and marbled sinks, I looked completely out of place. What was I doing here? What was our family doing in the Lakeview restaurant? In America?

The door to the ladies' room opened. A woman came in and glanced curiously at me. I retreated into one of the toilet cubicles and latched the door.

Time passed—maybe half an hour, maybe an hour. Then I heard the door open again, and my mother's voice. "Are you in there? You're not sick, are you?"

There was real concern in her voice. A girl can't leave her family just because they slurp their soup. Besides, the toilet cubicle had a few drawbacks as a permanent residence. "I'm all right," I said, undoing the latch.

Mother didn't tell me how the rest of the dinner went, and I didn't want to know. In the weeks following, I managed to push the whole thing into the back of my mind, where it jumped out at me only a few times a day. Even now, I turn hot all over when I think of the Lakeview restaurant.

But by the time we had been in this country for three months, our family was definitely making progress toward becoming Americanized. I remember my parents' first PTA meeting. Father wore a neat suit and tie, and Mother put on her first pair of high heels. She stumbled only once. They met my homeroom teacher and beamed as she told them that I would make honor roll soon at the rate I was going. Of course Chinese etiquette forced Father to say that I was a very stupid girl and Mother to protest that the teacher was showing favoritism toward me. But I could tell they were both very proud.

The day came when my parents announced that they wanted to give a dinner party. We had invited Chinese friends to eat with us before, but this dinner was going to be different. In addition to a Chinese-American family, we were going to invite the Gleasons.

"Gee, I can hardly wait to have dinner at your house," Meg said to me. "I just *love* Chinese food."

That was a relief. Mother was a good cook, but I wasn't sure if people who ate sour cream would also eat chicken gizzards stewed in soy sauce.

Mother decided not to take a chance with chicken gizzards. Since we had western guests, she set the table with large dinner plates, which we never used in Chinese meals. In fact we didn't use individual plates at all, but picked up food from the platters in the middle of the table and brought it directly to our rice bowls. Following the practice of Chinese-American restaurants, Mother also placed large serving spoons on the platters.

The dinner started well. Mrs. Gleason exclaimed at the beautifully arranged dishes of food: the colorful candied fruit in the sweet-and-sour pork dish, the noodle-thin shreds of chicken meat stir-fried with tiny peas, and the glistening pink prawns in a ginger sauce.

At first I was too busy enjoying my food to notice how the guests were doing. But soon I remembered my duties. Sometimes guests were too polite to help themselves and you had to serve them with more food.

I glanced at Meg, to see if she needed more food, and my eyes nearly popped out at the sight of her plate. It was piled with food: the sweet-and-sour meat pushed right against the chicken shreds, and the chicken sauce ran into the prawns. She had been taking food from a second dish before she finished eating her helping from the first!

Horrified, I turned to look at Mrs. Gleason. She was

dumping rice out of her bowl and putting it on her dinner plate. Then she ladled prawns and gravy on top of the rice and mixed everything together, the way you mix sand, gravel, and cement to make concrete.

I couldn't bear to look any longer, and I turned to Mr. Gleason. He was chasing a pea around his plate. Several times he got it to the edge, but when he tried to pick it up with his chopsticks, it rolled back toward the center of the plate again. Finally he put down his chopsticks and picked up the pea with his fingers. He really did! A grown man!

All of us, our family and the Chinese guests, stopped eating to watch the activities of the Gleasons. I wanted to giggle. Then I caught my mother's eyes on me. She frowned and shook her head slightly, and I understood the message: the Gleasons were not used to Chinese ways, and they were just coping the best they could. For some reason I thought of celery strings.

When the main courses were finished, Mother brought out a platter of fruit. "I hope you weren't expecting a sweet dessert," she said. "Since the Chinese don't eat dessert, I didn't think to prepare any."

"Oh, I couldn't possibly eat dessert!" cried Mrs. Gleason. "I'm simply stuffed!"

Meg had different ideas. When the table was cleared, she announced that she and I were going for a walk. "I don't know about you, but I feel like dessert," she told me, when we were outside. "Come on, there's a Dairy Queen down the street. I could use a big chocolate milkshake!"

Although I didn't really want anything more to eat, I insisted on paying for the milkshakes. After all, I was still hostess.

Meg got her large chocolate milkshake and I had a small one. Even so, she was finishing hers while I was only half done. Toward the end she pulled hard on her straws and went *shloop, shloop*.

"Do you always slurp when you eat a milkshake?" I asked, before I could stop myself.

Meg grinned. "Sure. All Americans slurp."

# August 2026:
# There Will Come Soft Rains

Ray Bradbury

In the living room the voice-clock sang, *Tick-tock, seven o'clock, time to get up, time to get up, seven o'clock!* as if it were afraid that nobody would. The morning house lay empty. The clock ticked on, repeating and repeating its sounds into the emptiness. *Seven-nine, breakfast time, seven-nine!*

In the kitchen the breakfast stove gave a hissing sigh and ejected from its warm interior eight pieces of perfectly browned toast, eight eggs sunnyside up, sixteen slices of bacon, two coffees, and two cool glasses of milk.

"Today is August 4, 2026," said a second voice from the kitchen ceiling, "in the city of Allendale, California." It repeated the date three times for memory's sake. "Today is Mr. Featherstone's birthday. Today is the anniversary of Tilita's marriage. Insurance is payable, as are the water, gas, and light bills."

Somewhere in the walls, relays clicked, memory tapes

glided under electric eyes.

*Eight-one, tick-tock, eight-one o'clock, off to school, off to work, run, run, eight-one!* But no doors slammed, no carpets took the soft tread of rubber heels. It was raining outside. The weather box on the front door sang quietly: "Rain, rain, go away; rubbers, raincoats for today . . ." And the rain tapped on the empty house, echoing.

Outside, the garage chimed and lifted its door to reveal the waiting car. After a long wait the door swung down again.

At eight-thirty the eggs were shriveled and the toast was like stone. An aluminum wedge scraped them into the sink, where hot water whirled them down a metal throat which digested and flushed them away to the distant sea. The dirty dishes were dropped into a hot washer and emerged twinkling dry.

*Nine-fifteen*, sang the clock, *time to clean.*

Out of warrens in the wall, tiny robot mice darted. The rooms were acrawl with the small cleaning animals, all rubber and metal. They thudded against chairs, whirling their mustached runners, kneading the rug nap, sucking gently at hidden dust. Then, like mysterious invaders, they popped into their burrows. Their pink electric eyes faded. The house was clean.

*Ten o'clock*. The sun came out from behind the rain. The house stood alone in a city of rubble and ashes. This was the one house left standing. At night the ruined city gave off a radioactive glow which could be seen for miles.

*Ten-fifteen*. The garden sprinklers whirled up in golden founts, filling the soft morning air with scatterings of brightness. The water pelted windowpanes, running down the charred west side where the house had been burned evenly free of its white paint. The entire west face of the house was black, save for five places. Here the silhouette in paint of a man mowing a lawn. Here, as in a photograph, a woman bent to pick flowers. Still farther over, their images burned on wood in one titanic instant, a small boy, hands flung into the air; higher up, the image of a thrown ball, and opposite him a girl, hands raised to catch a ball which never came down.

The five spots of paint—the man, the woman, the children, the ball—remained. The rest was a thin charcoaled layer.

The gentle sprinkler rain filled the garden with falling light.

Until this day, how well the house had kept its peace. How carefully it had inquired, "Who goes there? What's the password?" and, getting no answer from lonely foxes and whining cats, it had shut up its windows and drawn shades in an old-maidenly preoccupation with self-protection which bordered on a mechanical paranoia.

It quivered at each sound, the house did. If a sparrow brushed a window, the shade snapped up. The bird, startled, flew off! No, not even a bird must touch the house!

The house was an altar with ten thousand attendants, big, small, servicing, attending, in choirs. But the gods had gone away, and the ritual of the religion continued senselessly, uselessly.

*Twelve noon.*

A dog whined, shivering, on the front porch.

The front door recognized the dog voice and opened. The dog, once huge and fleshy, but now gone to bone and covered with sores, moved in and through the house, tracking mud. Behind it whirred angry mice, angry at having to pick up mud, angry at inconvenience.

For not a leaf fragment blew under the door but what the wall panels flipped open and the copper scrap rats flashed swiftly out. The offending dust, hair, or paper, seized in miniature steel jaws, was raced back to the burrows. There, down tubes which fed into the cellar, it was dropped into the sighing vent of an incinerator which sat like evil Baal in a dark corner.

The dog ran upstairs, hysterically yelping to each door, at last realizing, as the house realized, that only silence was here.

It sniffed the air and scratched the kitchen door. Behind the door, the stove was making pancakes which filled the house with a rich baked odor and the scent of maple syrup.

The dog frothed at the mouth, lying at the door, sniffing, its eyes turned to fire. It ran wildly in circles, biting at its tail, spun in a frenzy, and died. It lay in the parlor for an hour.

*Two o'clock*, sang a voice.

Delicately sensing decay at last, the regiments of mice hummed out as softly as blown gray leaves in an electrical wind.

*Two-fifteen.*

The dog was gone.

In the cellar, the incinerator glowed suddenly and a whirl of sparks leaped up the chimney.

*Two thirty-five.*

Bridge tables sprouted from patio walls. Playing cards fluttered onto pads in a shower of pips. Martinis manifested on an oaken bench with egg-salad sandwiches. Music played.

But the tables were silent and the cards untouched.

At four o'clock the tables folded like great butterflies back through the paneled walls.

*Four-thirty.*

The nursery walls glowed.

Animals took shape: yellow giraffes, blue lions, pink

antelopes, lilac panthers cavorting in crystal substance. The walls were glass. They looked out upon color and fantasy. Hidden films clocked through well-oiled sprockets, and the walls lived. The nursery floor was woven to resemble a crisp, cereal meadow. Over this ran aluminum roaches and iron crickets, and in the hot still air butterflies of delicate red tissue wavered among the sharp aroma of animal spoors! There was the sound like a great matted yellow hive of bees within a dark bellows, the lazy bumble of a purring lion. And there was the patter of okapi feet and the murmur of a fresh jungle rain, like other hoofs, falling upon the sum-mer-starched grass. Now the walls dissolved into distances of parched weed, mile on mile, and warm endless sky. The animals drew away into thorn brakes and water holes.

It was the children's hour.

*Five o'clock.* The bath filled with clear hot water.

*Six, seven, eight o'clock.* The dinner dishes manipu-lated like magic tricks, and in the study a *click.* In the metal stand opposite the hearth where a fire now blazed up warmly, a cigar popped out, half an inch of soft gray ash on it, smoking, waiting.

*Nine o'clock.* The beds warmed their hidden circuits, for nights were cool here.

*Nine-five.* A voice spoke from the study ceiling:

"Mrs. McClellan, which poem would you like this evening?"

The house was silent.

The voice said at last, "Since you express no prefer-ence, I shall select a poem at random." Quiet music rose to back the voice. "Sara Teasdale. As I recall, your favorite. . . .

There will come soft rains and the smell of the ground,
And swallows circling with their shimmering sound;

And frogs in the pools singing at night,
And wild plum trees in tremulous white;

Robins will wear their feathery fire,
Whistling their whims on a low fence-wire;

And not one will know of the war, not one
Will care at last when it is done.

Not one would mind, neither bird nor tree,
If mankind perished utterly;

And Spring herself, when she woke at dawn
Would scarcely know that we were gone.

The fire burned on the stone hearth and the cigar fell away into a mound of quiet ash on its tray. The empty chairs faced each other between the silent walls, and the music played.

At ten o'clock the house began to die.

The wind blew. A falling tree bough crashed through the kitchen window. Cleaning solvent, bottled, shattered over the stove. The room was ablaze in an instant!

"Fire!" screamed a voice. The house lights flashed, water pumps shot water from the ceilings. But the solvent spread on the linoleum, licking, eating, under the kitchen door, while the voices took it up in chorus: "Fire, fire, fire!"

The house tried to save itself. Doors sprang tightly shut, but the windows were broken by the heat and the wind blew and sucked upon the fire.

The house gave ground as the fire in ten billion angry sparks moved with flaming ease from room to room and then up the stairs. While scurrying water rats squeaked from the walls, pistoled their water, and ran for more. And the wall sprays let down showers of mechanical rain.

But too late. Somewhere, sighing, a pump shrugged to a stop. The quenching rain ceased. The reserve water supply which had filled baths and washed dishes for many quiet days was gone.

The fire crackled up the stairs. It fed upon Picassos and Matisses in the upper halls, like delicacies, baking off the oily flesh, tenderly crisping the canvases into black shavings.

Now the fire lay in beds, stood in windows, changed the colors of drapes!

And then, reinforcements.

From attic trapdoors, blind robot faces peered down with faucet mouths gushing green chemical.

The fire backed off, as even an elephant must at the sight of a dead snake. Now there were twenty snakes whipping over the floor, killing the fire with a clear cold venom of green froth.

But the fire was clever. It had sent flames outside the house, up through the attic to the pumps there. An explosion! The attic brain which directed the pumps was shattered into bronze shrapnel on the beams.

The fire rushed back into every closet and felt of the clothes hung there.

The house shuddered, oak bone on bone, its bared skeleton cringing from the heat, its wire, its nerves revealed as if a surgeon had torn the skin off to let the red veins and capillaries quiver in the scalded air. Help, help! Fire! Run, run! Heat snapped mirrors like the brittle winter ice. And the voices wailed Fire, fire, run, run, like a tragic nursery rhyme, a dozen voices, high, low, like children dying in a forest, alone, alone. And the voices fading as the wires popped their sheathings like hot chestnuts. One, two, three, four, five voices died.

In the nursery the jungle burned. Blue lions roared,

purple giraffes bounded off. The panthers ran in circles, changing color, and ten million animals, running before the fire, vanished off toward a distant steaming river. . . .

Ten more voices died. In the last instant under the fire avalanche, other choruses, oblivious, could be heard announcing the time, playing music, cutting the lawn by remote-control mower, or setting an umbrella frantically out and in the slamming and opening front door, a thousand things happening, like a clock shop when each clock strikes the hour insanely before or after the other, a scene of maniac confusion, yet unity; singing, screaming, a few last cleaning mice darting bravely out to carry the horrid ashes away! And one voice, with sublime disregard for the situation, read poetry aloud in the fiery study, until all the film spools burned, until all the wires withered and the circuits cracked.

The fire burst the house and let it slam flat down, puffing out skirts of spark and smoke.

In the kitchen, an instant before the rain of fire and timber, the stove could be seen making breakfasts at a psychopathic rate, ten dozen eggs, six loaves of toast, twenty dozen bacon strips, which, eaten by fire, started the stove working again, hysterically hissing!

The crash. The attic smashing into kitchen and parlor. The parlor into cellar, cellar into sub-cellar. Deep freeze, armchair, film tapes, circuits, beds, and all like skeletons thrown in a cluttered mound deep under.

Smoke and silence. A great quantity of smoke.

Dawn showed faintly in the east. Among the ruins, one wall stood alone. Within the wall, a last voice said, over and over again and again, even as the sun rose to shine upon the heaped rubble and steam:

"Today is August 5, 2026, today is August 5, 2026, today is . . ."

# LAND OF TRASH

Ian Tamblyn

## CHARACTERS

NUKE: a young street kid
STRYDER: another street kid
CARSON: an old mutant living in a trash dump

## SCENE 1

(*Lights down. Distant barking. Dogs on trail of something, their sounds getting closer.* CARSON *has hidden in some of the trash on stage. Just as dogs sound as if they are about to pounce on the audience, the doors near the stage burst open,* STRYDER *and* NUKE *race around the audience and 'set' on their bikes.*)

STRYDER. Nix on phalt path! Down get here! Nuke!—down get here! Quick!

NUKE (*in pain*). Can't down get! Tired I! Stomach is a stitch! . . . I . . .

STRYDER. Use inhaler! You can do! Stash bike . . . the dogs. The dogs!

**Nuke.** Coming! See dogs on hill . . . dogs on hill!

**Stryder.** Know I. Trackers with them?

**Nuke.** No—jus dogs. . . . Bulls!

**Stryder.** Quick!

**Nuke.** Should no leave bikes here!

**Stryder.** Back for bikes—they no find. Stash bikes. Lose dogs now! What be real. There! Stash bikes. They no find. Run sewage lagoon. We cross there! Dogs no come. Hide us in trash . . . you make it?

**Nuke.** Yeah—I be o.k. You see dogs?

**Stryder** (*laughing*). Yeah—nosing the lagoon. Lost in bigger smells. We got 'em!

**Nuke.** Good. Still no Trackers?

**Stryder.** No. Jus dogs. Turning back now—we safe.

**Nuke.** Was close.

**Stryder.** Was close but Stryder and Nuke too tough for Trackers—fact.

**Nuke.** Total fact.

**Stryder.** Watch you see?

**Nuke.** Too high! Everything reading high—PCBs . . . Dioxins . . . FURans . . . why this dump open—still too hot! This dump still hot. Too dangerous. We split!

**Stryder.** No! We here now! They say dump re-open for trashers. Seventy-five-year limit. They say!

**Nuke.** They say! How many times they say—and they be wrong! We go!

**Stryder.** No! We here. We first in this dump for trades. We be thick in the best trades. Without trades we no eat, be a fact.

**Nuke.** Jamming this dump be bad news Stryder! Look— check out levels—out of control! You 'n me, our control be high already, we get disease. We go—o.k.?

**Stryder.** Go? Where? Back to dogs! No. Got to work this dump, we need trades Nuke, that a fact.

NUKE. Fact.

STRYDER. No good—no choice. Check it out.

NUKE. Your show. Be I check it out! Strange world. No
'nize no thing here. Extreme old dump Stryder. Wow!
Look over there—old technotrash! Stryder, this be
before meltdowns!

STRYDER. What I say! Old world dump. Be our first.
Excellent trades here Nuke, we be thick in trades.
Fossil fuel cars, computers, digitals, electronics . . .

NUKE. Chemicals . . .

STRYDER. Back off! Be here now. Keep counter on—we
stay clear of chemical soup.

NUKE. Be a plan, but we thick in soup.

(NUKE *and* STRYDER *poke through the set of garbage,*
*familiar to the audience, but mysterious to them.*
*They are perplexed by everything they see.* STRYDER
*picks up an old transistor radio.*)

STRYDER. What be?

NUKE. No know . . .

STRYDER. Transmitter some kind? Got antennae. Sus this
numbers cross front.

NUKE. Hmm, never seen. Check inside—primitive circuit.
Ancient. Something though.

STRYDER. What be? (*pause*) Memory. Was old guy walkin'
streets. Was flipped but sang . . . songs. Noises.
Yeah—he listened to noises on Radians. Radians! was
what it was! Old guy sang song go "at McDonald's". . .
something like that—no know. He say Radian songs
no more. System take over communications. No use
now. (STRYDER *throws radio away.*)

NUKE. No—I fix! We listen to the System transmissions.
We be head of Trackers.

STRYDER. Good head glow!—you still strong upstairs!
(STRYDER *retrieves radio and they continue to sift*

*through junk.* STRYDER *mumbles the line . . . "at McDonald's" . . . but only that part of the melody. From back of stage a hubcap is tossed landing near* STRYDER *and* NUKE. *They immediately go into alert, defensive stance.*)

STRYDER. What be?

NUKE. No know—we split!

STRYDER. No! We stay. Maybe rat knock something.

NUKE. Tracker dog?

STRYDER. Doubt—they come straight for . . .

(*Another noise is made offstage.*)

NUKE. There!

STRYDER. Mutant?

NUKE. No see. If dump open, Mutant no be here. They only allowed hot dumps.

STRYDER. Maybe this Mutant no know this dump open. Be the wolf.

NUKE. I the wolf.

(CARSON *enters, limping, very angry.*)

CARSON. Get out of my dump! Little punks—get out!

STRYDER. Is Mutant! Careful!

NUKE. Split! Back to bikes! Quick!

STRYDER. No! Dogs back there . . . wait a minute.

CARSON. Little worms! You hear me, I said get outta here! Now!

NUKE. He disease.

STRYDER. Fact. Weak—take him out easy. See what he say.

NUKE. You crazy!

STRYDER. So say they! Time for a tease . . .

CARSON. You don't hear do you. I said . . .

STRYDER. We heard old man. Stand back. We cut you down.

CARSON. What's the matter? Are you afraid of a sick old man with a little . . . INFECTION! (*He lunges at them.* STRYDER *and* NUKE *jump back.*)

STRYDER. Back off! Report you to Quarantines.

CARSON. You won't report me to Quarantines, kid. They're after you for something already. I saw the dogs.

NUKE. You disease. We get word in.

CARSON. Quarantines. Ha! You think I'm afraid of Quarantines? What can they do to me that hasn't been done already?

STRYDER. Take you out. New law.

CARSON. Is that so? There's new laws every day—get out!

STRYDER. Not going. System post sign say this dump open. We here. For trades. You, Mutant, leave when dump opens. Know rule.

CARSON. "Know rule" . . . listen to you talk. What an abomination of the English language.

NUKE. Speak no in old way—no time.

CARSON. Pathetic. You're street kids, aren't you? You're runaways.

STRYDER. So?

CARSON. You kids are on the outside just like me!

NUKE. We no disease Mutant! We no sick!

CARSON. You will be . . . is it bad out there?

NUKE. All broke down since the floods, most of the city under.

CARSON. Where are your parents?

NUKE. Lost in floods, no find.

CARSON. I'm sorry.

NUKE. Sorry? About what? You know why he sorry Stryder?

STRYDER. No. Nuke. Watch his power. He pulling us in with his words. He trick us with feelings.

CARSON. What are you talking about? Don't you miss your parents?

STRYDER. NO! Drop subject! Look, Mutant . . .

CARSON. My name is Carson.

NUKE. CARSNO! CARSNOGENIC—Got a yok on it.

STRYDER. Look Carsno—needs we trades for food. Understand. Needs to work this dump. No trouble you.

CARSON. Fine. There's nothing I can do to stop you. You know about the chemicals here, I suppose?

NUKE. Seen 'em on counter.

CARSON. Yes, you see them on the counter, all right, but there are some things the counter doesn't read.

STRYDER. We know old man . . .

CARSON. Yeah, you punks know everything, don't you? Well stay away from this area over here. See the signs? Radioactive. (*laughs*) Stay away if you don't want to end up like me.

NUKE. Hey! Where you go?

STRYDER. Let him go—you fallin' for his power.

NUKE. How he live out here?

CARSON. What did you say?

NUKE. Nothing.

CARSON. Ha! I get by. A sick old man doesn't need much now, does he?

(CARSON *exits.*)

STRYDER. Why you talk to him so much?

NUKE. Wanted him close to get count on him. Meltdown victim. High radioactivity.

STRYDER. I sus. Nuke—no talk with him so much. You know he trap you with his language. Has power.

NUKE. You believe?

STRYDER. Fact.

NUKE. Very strange. Maybe power . . . maybe hidin' something. Feeling from sixth sense.

STRYDER. Felt that too. We sus.

NUKE. Why he let us stay?

STRYDER. He know we be right. Maybe soft.

NUKE. Says we be the same—both outside.

STRYDER. Fact. Very strange. No mind. Gots works. You be with counter, I be detector. Mine this joint.

(NUKE *turns on his chemical analyser, starts reading around the dump.*)

NUKE. No mine here Stryder . . . Dump full of chemicals, ground soaked—maximum danger, counter can't keep up . . . a Love Canal.

STRYDER. Stay on counter. I dig. This dump a goldmine, Nuke. Tons of stuff. Motors, medical, some very strange. Like no other dump seen before. Think, a goldmine!

NUKE. Some goldmine.

STRYDER. Why Mutant hang around here? Must be something keep him round.

NUKE. Maybe . . . something.

STRYDER. Come on—time for trades!

(NUKE *and* STRYDER *search through junk.* STRYDER *finds phone.*)

STRYDER. Hey Nuke, here! Found something!

NUKE. What be?

STRYDER. No know—get dirt off. Strange. Remember . . .

NUKE. 'Nother transmitter. Portable. Banned now. Only System use them now. Portable phone. Was in cars I think.

STRYDER. Car phone! Too much! How old?

NUKE. Cars banned in 2015 after second crisis, maybe 60 years. Maybe more.

STRYDER. Extreme. Take back—get going. We tap into line, cause all kinds of action.

NUKE. Get us killed, Stryder.

STRYDER. No way. Hey, something else down here. It got the sweats on it.

NUKE. What be?

STRYDER. No know . . . hey . . . be a pipe . . . pipe goes . . . this way . . . Nuke, check out.

NUKE. Pipe clean. It sweats.

STRYDER. Water! Be a water pipe, Nuke! We hit the jackpot! The Mutant's got water!

NUKE. Can't be. No clean water in dump, Stryder.

STRYDER. Check it out! Follow pipe . . . pipe go . . . come on . . . we follow pipe . . . Nuke?

NUKE. Can't believe—clean water . . . why . . .

STRYDER. The pipe . . . it goes . . . out of dump . . . look . . . it goes . . . up into hills.

NUKE. Right out of dump! You maybe right Stryder! Clean water!

(*They exit.* CARSON *re-enters, throws stuff over greenhouse, talking into it.*)

CARSON. When did they open the dump?! They didn't post a sign! I must do something to get rid of the Modems. They must not find you my precious. This place is mine! It belongs to me. Those Modems—festering rats. I've seen their kind before. They feel nothing, their feelings are dead. If only I could talk to them—No! I must get rid of them! They must not find you my hopefuls, they will destroy everything! Are you o.k.? I must think clearly . . . there, there, I must cover you up—there is danger near . . . yes my sweets, great danger. (CARSON *exits.*)

(STRYDER *and* NUKE *enter.*)

STRYDER. Major find Nuke!

NUKE. Total fact.

STRYDER. That be why Mutant here. He have himself a source. This be worth a goldmine. Knew there was something 'bout him.

NUKE. No clean water left outside System control. This be deep secret.

STRYDER. Nuke and Stryder secret!

NUKE. What?

STRYDER. We tap into line—fill jugs—this be the ticket Nuke . . . sell in streets. We never be hungry no more.

NUKE. We take water?

STRYDER. Fact. This our source, too.

NUKE. The Mutant . . .

STRYDER. Nix—nothing he can do! Who he tell?

NUKE. He take us out—this serious.

STRYDER. NO—Mutant soft inside. Can tell.

NUKE. You crazy, Stryder! Crazy!

STRYDER. So say they! Plan?

NUKE. Plan.

STRYDER. Fact! Sus out glass bottle—bottle—clean—plastic something. Tap into line with knife.

NUKE. Mutant with water—very rad. No thick.

STRYDER. No way—this Mutant got lights on.

NUKE. Stryder?

STRYDER. What say?

NUKE. What Mutant using water for? No selling water for sure . . .

STRYDER. Lights on Nuke . . . no know. He be up to something. We sus. Something going on. . . . Hey! Cut through! Ho! Water be . . . (STRYDER *has big reaction to the taste of the water, as if it was an elixir.*) Too much! Check it out . . .

(*laughing*) . . . it be clean water!

(NUKE *runs for jugs.* STRYDER *and* NUKE *both kneel down to gather drinking water. They do not see* CARSON *approaching.* CARSON *hits bucket with cane.* NUKE *and* STRYDER *look up to see* CARSON *holding a large iron bar over his head.*)

NUKE and STRYDER. No!

CARSON. You little punks, I warned you!

STRYDER. No touch—we're gone!

CARSON. I should have known . . . you are just like the rats around here. You can't help yourself, can you?

NUKE. We go! Back off!

CARSON. NOW!

STRYDER. We're history—relax, old man.

CARSON. Don't come back here.

NUKE. Oh—we come back.

CARSON. What?

STRYDER. You heard Mutant. We come back through System. They love to know. To horde a crime. To horde water a big crime—eh, Carsno?

CARSON. Why you little . . .

STRYDER. Stryder be my name. Say you what?

CARSON. Punks.

STRYDER. We be the street. No push the street. The street push back. You 'stand.

CARSON (*sarcastic*). I yes, I understand—you kids are a real threat! You've already told me I'm not supposed to be here so I'm gone—take the water—it's all yours.

STRYDER. Good. You see this thing clear.

CARSON. Yes—very clear. But maybe just because I don't want you or the System to have this water, just maybe I will contaminate it with disease and you won't know till it's too late! I could do that.

NUKE. No!

CARSON. Watch me! I can be the street too!

STRYDER. Fine! Good one Carsno! You got lights on—can see. Cut a deal?

CARSON. What kind of deal?

STRYDER. For water rights. You no pollute—we no report you to System. You live here—we no tell. Be fact—we hide you.

CARSON. Someone will find out . . .

STRYDER. Listen disease. You no pollute. We protect you. No one know. We trade clean water to streets. Be our ticket.

CARSON. Oh sure—water to the streets. Next thing you know everyone will be following you up here.

NUKE. We say we tapping System water. They leave us alone. Too frightened.

STRYDER. That's it! Nuke and I best survivors and best dodgers . . . no one find out. Deal?

CARSON. For now! But if anyone finds out about this water you know what I will do.

STRYDER. Fact. Grab jugs Nuke! We got our ticket!

CARSON. No! Wait! You must not cut my line with a knife! I'll set up a tap!

NUKE. You give us tap—we set up—you got sickness.

CARSON. Fine.

STRYDER. Deal?

CARSON. Deal— . . . no speak . . . oh my goodness, I'm beginning to talk like these fools.

NUKE. Big gamble Stryder . . . you pin him up.

STRYDER. That be plan but Mutant got the smarts.

NUKE. Serious contender, must watch close.

STRYDER. Don't go into him. Maximum danger.

NUKE. I watch.

STRYDER. I get bikes for transport, you come.

NUKE. I stay, fill jugs, you bikes . . .

STRYDER. Be a plan. Don't talk to him too much.

NUKE. No way.

STRYDER. I judge. Be gone.

(STRYDER *exits.* NUKE *filling jugs of water.*)

NUKE. Mutant have got smarts. What he be about with water. Find out . . . about him.

(CARSON *approaches* NUKE.)

NUKE. Stand back!

CARSON. I am not going to touch you! Careful—that one had cleaning solvent in it.

NUKE. Fact.

(*silence*)

CARSON. It's just not the disease you're afraid of is it? There's something else . . .

NUKE. Not afraid—some say old ways have power—no believe.

CARSON. We have a power? That's a good one. I don't think we have any power at all. If I had any power . . .

NUKE. Carson?

CARSON. Yes?

NUKE. What happen?

CARSON. To what?

NUKE. This.

CARSON. You don't know?

NUKE. Know story. Know what we got. World change. Heat go up. Brown clouds come. Eating rain fall. Meltdowns. Floods come. Cities drown. Everything breakdown.

CARSON. Yep—you've got it right—that's pretty well how it went.

NUKE. No! That be a story. What be real? Want to know what happened.

CARSON. Why?—it's all gone!—your story says it all—it happened so fast.

NUKE. Tell me.

CARSON. I don't know. I've had a lifetime to see the changes and I don't believe it myself. We just didn't know it would come so fast . . .

NUKE. Old man! You mumble like everyone else!

CARSON. All right! We took too much from the earth and never gave anything back. No—that's not quite right. We put things back, into the air, on the land and in the water, but most of it was bad. We thought we could go on taking forever, that the world would always give us more, but of course we were wrong. We were killing the planet. The heat built up first . . .

NUKE. No more!

CARSON. Why?—you asked me to explain?

NUKE. I hear! How could you let this be—you knew!

CARSON. Yes, we knew—but we didn't believe it was happening. We did not see the world as a living, breathing thing. We thought we could just take more and more and it would go on forever. And everybody wanted more. There were some early warnings and at the turn of the last century, there was some concern, but it was almost like a fad. You see, at that time everybody talked about the environment and everybody said that there had to be a change, but in the end nobody really did much of anything. You see, people just weren't prepared to give up the very things that were causing the problem. No one believed we would actually have to give up *anything*.

NUKE. Carson! My point be—you knew! You could have made a change! Floods, disease, killing rain, didn't have to be!

CARSON. Yes—it didn't have to be. We could have saved the planet, but we couldn't give up our toys. Then—it was too late and the change came so fast.

NUKE. Now everything gone. Everything grey. We live in ruins of what was. World be dead. Story called "The Taking."

CARSON. I'm afraid so.

(*silence*)

CARSON. Nuke?—is that your name?

NUKE. Yeah . . . be my name.

CARSON. Can you tell me something?

NUKE. What be?

CARSON. The cities? What has happened there? Mutants have been banned for twenty years. I would like to know.

NUKE. No. You no want to know. But I tell. Water up twenty-five feet so say. Too many people crowd above waterline. More come every day. Little food. Disease. Say System control but that no be. They control what be left. Supplies, food, guns. System be corrupt. Serve themselves. Be a war to survive.

CARSON. Picking through dumps is how you survive?

NUKE. You got a problem. Trades for food. Be all.

(NUKE *turns away from* CARSON.)

CARSON. Hey!—what are you doing? We were having a conversation!

NUKE. We talk too much—Stryder!

STRYDER (*comes in with bikes*). What be?

NUKE. Was slippin' in.

STRYDER. Carsno! You back off! Now!

CARSON. I was. . . . What's going on here!? This is my home, not yours. I just let you take my precious . . .

STRYDER. This be your home!—this land of trash! Some home!

CARSON. Why you!

STRYDER. Too many questions! Leave Nuke be!

CARSON. He was asking me!!! I just asked about the city.

STRYDER. No mind! I tell you. Story go—this ting we got no need be. Story go—you turned world against itself. Story go—you push it—it push back. Story go—you keep pushing. Story go—like that, Mutant—so what you need to know? Eh!

CARSON. No—it wasn't me. I was against it all . . . you must understand!

STRYDER. Understand. You did no ting. Where's the world

you had? All gone! All gone! Where's animals, fish, forests, all gone! All gone. What you do?

CARSON. I . . .

STRYDER. Come on, Nuke! I show him power of word! Choke in throat . . . but, say they all! Take water with no thanks—the least we get from this land of trash! Come on, Nuke!

(STRYDER *and* NUKE *leave on bikes laden down with water jugs.* CARSON *is left staring at them centre stage.*)

(*Music cue.*)

# Scene 2

NUKE. Dogs? See you dogs?

STRYDER. Nix—Trackers 'n dogs long gone. Ace move Nuke.

NUKE. Radian transmitter work fine with solder 'n batteries. We got a fix on Trackers, no problem.

STRYDER. Got 'm beat for good. Good head glow.

NUKE. Light go on another way.

STRYDER. What be?

NUKE. Thinking water not the total picture.

STRYDER. Fact. Thinking he be hiding something else.

NUKE. Could be he throw us off with water. Easy gift. Water for something.

STRYDER. Be my thought. We check out. Find his treasure.

(CARSON *suddenly reappears.*)

CARSON. Treasure! What treasure?

STRYDER. Oh! No treasure, I mean treasure be water . . .

NUKE. Come back for more . . .

CARSON. I see . . . more water . . .

NUKE. More water . . .

STRYDER. Yeah—sold all water for trades—everyone wants water. We be a hit!

NUKE. Carson?

CARSON. Yes?

NUKE. What was it like before the change?

STRYDER. Nuke!

NUKE. Take him off . . .

STRYDER. Sus.

CARSON. What's going on here? What are you two whispering about?

NUKE. Nothing. Stryder fears your language. Old language has power so say. I no feared of language.

CARSON. I should say not, the way you torture it. You Modems think we have power in our language? How strange! I thought we had lost all power. Now what were you asking me?

NUKE. What was it like before the change?

CARSON. Where's your friend going?

NUKE. Jugs. Need more jugs.

CARSON. I see . . . well . . . what?

NUKE. The change . . .

CARSON (*suspicious*). Why are you so interested in the past? Are you just toying with an old man? Eh?

NUKE. No. Someone must remember. The street don't care.

CARSON. But you ask and then you get frightened. What are you frightened of?

NUKE. The colour of your language—too strong for a grey world.

(*several beats*)

CARSON. I understand. Are you sure you want to hear? The past. The world was a beautiful place. Cold, crisp days in winter, the lakes froze and white snow fell. Spring was rich with the smell of the warming earth and everything was full of life. Soon, the sweet fragrances of summer flowers would mingle in the air and dance with the fireflies at night.

NUKE. What's a firefly?

CARSON. A tiny insect that could glow in the dark, like miniature stars . . . I haven't seen a firefly in forty years . . .

NUKE. See no more.

CARSON. No. (*pause*) I miss the fall. Great wedges of geese flying down from the north, the trees aflame with colour.

NUKE. Trees burned in fall?

CARSON. No (*laughs*). Well, in a way. How could you know? Nuke, the leaves changed colour in fall. The maple trees turned scarlet and crimson; the aspen, a breathtaking gold; some oak turned almost purple. The leaves fell and formed a thick carpet on the forest floor.

NUKE. What be L-Phant?

CARSON. Elephant? Oh, it was the largest land animal. It had long tusks and a longer nose they called a trunk, big ears and . . .

NUKE. Yeah! And what be a Hypobottomus?

CARSON (*laughing*). That's a Hippopotamus! They were big too, lived in the rivers like the Nile in Africa.

NUKE. All gone?

CARSON. All gone.

NUKE. Whales. Tell me whales!

CARSON. Whales were beautiful. The Blue Whale was the biggest animal the world has ever known.

NUKE. Bigger than a dinosaur?

CARSON. Yes. The Blue Whale could be eighty to a hundred feet long. It was . . .

NUKE. No more!

CARSON. What's wrong? What did I say?

NUKE. Story too rich.

CARSON. Language was meant to be rich.

NUKE. Language has a memory? Stryder! Memory be the power.

STRYDER. Nuke!

NUKE. Come! Get me away!

(STRYDER *runs onto set.*)

STRYDER. You be?

NUKE. Falling in again—take me away.

STRYDER. Did good—throw him off me—found something.

NUKE. He gets me. He pulls tears from me.

STRYDER. Told you—he has powers.

CARSON (*to himself*). I meant no harm. I didn't know I could affect him.

STRYDER. Stop! You know what be a spark. You play game of memories. Keep memories to yourself, old man—the past is dead. Nuke—we go back to streets. You ride?

NUKE. Yeah—I ride.

(NUKE *and* STRYDER *exit.*)

CARSON. That Stryder is up to something . . . while I was talking to Nuke . . .

(*Cut to* NUKE *and* STRYDER.)

STRYDER. Did good Nuke! You be o.k.?

NUKE. The story of the flaming trees . . .

STRYDER. Why you listen? Stories afore change more dangerous than chemicals.

NUKE. Said world was beautiful.

STRYDER. Don't believe what he say! You go soft on him.

NUKE. I want to know what was.

STRYDER. What was long gone—no look back now. You throw him off be fine, but don't fall in.

NUKE. No fall. What you find?

STRYDER. Mutant got pipes all kinds joining—all go to different piles of junk.

(NUKE *and* STRYDER *exit. Theme music.*)

# Scene 3

*(Darkness in the junk yard.* NUKE *and* STRYDER *with headlamps, searching.)*

STRYDER. Nuke!

NUKE. Yeah?

STRYDER. You ready?

NUKE. Yep. Ready.

STRYDER. Be the wolf.

NUKE. Stryder?

STRYDER. What?

NUKE. No harm Mutant . . .

STRYDER. You soft on disease man?

NUKE. No. I . . . Mutant give us water ticket, be all.

STRYDER. You fall in too much—give us this mess.

NUKE. Fact . . .

STRYDER. Leave Mutant alone, he leave us alone. Go!

NUKE. Gone.

STRYDER. Find the line?

NUKE. Everything move! Mutant make a change!

STRYDER. On to us! Must be hiding treasure! Use detector!

NUKE. Nix. Make a noise.

STRYDER. Fact. Was over here?

NUKE. Thinking so . . . . Got it. Find line.

STRYDER. Total. Stop. Make a plan.

NUKE. You a plan?

STRYDER. You follow line—I sus Mutant. Give signal if find. Make like back for . . . detector . . . left detector . . . he no sus.

NUKE. Perfect. I gone.

STRYDER. Luck.

(NUKE *crawls behind junk*.)

STRYDER. Treasure. What be treasure? Treasure in a junk
pile. Treasure in a ruin. Be a joke. Thinking we don't
know this mess a mess. Six sense know was different.
Six sense know a different world. No need fall into
words. Was trees, was birds, was whales, was days
without clouds. Light inside remember. Now Nuke and
Stryder rats in a dump. Be us all. So give us treasure!

(NUKE *signals*. STRYDER *rushes over to a pile of junk*
*covering greenhouse*.)

STRYDER. What you sus?

NUKE. Line lead here.

STRYDER. Clear junk . . . something inside.

NUKE. Wait! Radioactive sign. No glow here.

(NUKE *uncovers greenhouse*.)

NUKE. Wrong! Is glow inside. Look.

STRYDER. Fact. What be? . . . what be?!

(STRYDER *rips away junk*. NUKE *and* STRYDER *peer*
*into greenhouse*. *Greenhouse lights come on*.)

NUKE. Stryder, look!

STRYDER. Outside!

(NUKE *and* STRYDER *stare at greenhouse world in dis-*
*belief*.)

STRYDER. Be a world within a world . . .

NUKE. Be a green house . . .

STRYDER. All the colours . . .

NUKE. Be all the colours of the stories. Look! Stryder!
Something hop in corner!

STRYDER. Where? What be?

NUKE. Under leaf! There! It hop!

STRYDER. See! What be?

NUKE. Fr . . . Fr . . . Frog!

**STRYDER.** What be a frog!

**NUKE.** No know. Never see—only hear.

**STRYDER.** Never see such beauty.

**NUKE.** This was world. Oh look!—something fly with big wings all colours—all too much!

**STRYDER.** Big hit for eyes, Nuke—be careful. What we do?

**NUKE.** No know—no wonder Carson hide this. Too much. All these things gone.

**STRYDER.** Fact. We looking back afore change. Never thought this.

**NUKE.** Stories be true. We leave alone. Too big.

**STRYDER.** No! Light go on!

**NUKE.** What be?

**STRYDER.** Light go on! Where's Mutant? Where's Carsno?

**NUKE.** What's up? Carson no around. Why you turn away?

**STRYDER.** Too much power in my eyes.

**NUKE.** We go . . . we leave alone.

**STRYDER.** No! No get lost in wonder. We start our own— garden.

**NUKE.** Take his world! No way! We can't do that Stryder! We can't take his world!

**STRYDER.** Our ticket!

**NUKE.** No!

**STRYDER.** No guts.

**NUKE.** No. This be what they did. The taking. We can't do this no more! You push—it push back, remember Stryder! They die out there!

**STRYDER.** No! This be not the taking. Be the taking back!

**NUKE.** Not right!

**STRYDER.** So say! I say you soft on Mutant. Gone in. Plants maximum trades, you be for or against?

**NUKE.** Extreme against . . . but we blood.

STRYDER. Fact. How we take?

NUKE. Be your show.

STRYDER. Fact. Get bag, quick.

(NUKE *looks for bag.*)

STRYDER. Little world. All the colours, never seen.

(NUKE *comes back with bag.*)

STRYDER. We take back in this.

NUKE. You say . . .

STRYDER. That one. Take that one. Flower?

NUKE. Oh Stryder! Take care! No kill!

STRYDER. No problem. Into sack little world, new home.
Quick—split outta here—bikes?

(*They turn to meet* CARSON, *He is coming for them.*)

CARSON (*with controlled rage*). Put the plant back!

STRYDER. Mutant!—split up—street plan—Go!

NUKE. Leave plant!

STRYDER. No!

CARSON. Come back! It will die out there!

(CARSON *chases after* STRYDER *but she is too fast.*
*Chase continues around the dump. Plant is often in*
*danger. Finally,* CARSON *traps* NUKE.)

CARSON. So! It's come to this, has it?

NUKE. Was not . . .

CARSON. Don't tell me you weren't part of this. Call Stryder back now!

NUKE. I can't . . .

CARSON. You want to look like me, Nuke? You want to
be banished like me? I'll give you the touch!

NUKE. No . . . please . . .

CARSON. Then call her back. Now!

NUKE. Stryder! Where you be?

(*silence*)

NUKE. Stryder! Mutant got me! Come!

STRYDER. Nuke?

CARSON. Tell her to bring the plant back.

NUKE. Stryder! Quick! Bring plant! He give me the touch!

CARSON. Now, we'll see what kind of friend the street makes! I should have known you couldn't just settle for the water. Always more, always more!

NUKE. Not my idea . . .

CARSON. Your tough friend, eh? Where's your tough friend now?

(STRYDER *returns from behind* CARSON *and* NUKE.)

STRYDER (*calmly*). I'm here.

CARSON. My plant. Give it back! I want my . . .

STRYDER. Shut up! Let Nuke go—you get plant!

CARSON. No! I'm not that much a fool! You'll pull some kind of trick. I want the plant back in the greenhouse or your friend gets the touch!

NUKE. Stryder—play straight—Mutant over edge—mean what he say!

CARSON. Those plants are everything to me!

STRYDER. You no let one plant go?

CARSON. No! They will die out there! You don't know how to take care of them!

STRYDER. No tell me of caretaking!—look around, be the care you take!

CARSON. No! I fought against them all! I saw the world turning—I did all I could to stop the madness, the greed!

STRYDER. Well, old man, I guess you didn't fight enough, and now you disease Nuke for one plant. You still don't know eh, Carsno?

CARSON. No! You have it wrong. I must save what little there is left. The plants must come first now—it is *you* Stryder that has not changed. You continue to take! I can't allow this. It is my last fight.

STRYDER. I understand. You no give us something that

lives—you gives us a land of trash. Here be plant. Luck. (STRYDER *tosses the plant high in the air.* CARSON *looks up to catch it.* NUKE *escapes. As* CARSON *is about to catch the plant,* STRYDER *knocks him over with metal detector.* STRYDER *grabs plant. They run.* CARSON *chases after them.*)

CARSON. Please! Don't take my precious away!

STRYDER. Yesterday's news old man, we're gone!

(*As* STRYDER *is about to take off on bike,* NUKE *stops.* CARSON *catches up but holds back.*)

STRYDER. Come on Nuke! Got him beat!

NUKE. It won't work.

STRYDER. What no work? Come on!

NUKE. No Stryder—no run. No sense.

STRYDER. What are you talking now?

NUKE. What we doing? Where we run? So we got plant—one more thing, like other things, probably die like he say . . .

STRYDER. No!

NUKE. Yes. Listen. We run all the time. We run now. Where to? Back to streets, back to dogs. No more.

STRYDER. No stand you . . .

NUKE. We be running from the wrong place. We stay here.

CARSON. What are you talking about?

NUKE. Stay here with you Carson—help you out.

STRYDER. You gone over! Nuke!

CARSON. Stay here—help?

NUKE. Yeah—you no live forever. Who look after green world when you're gone . . .

CARSON. I hadn't thought that far. You would stay and build with me?

NUKE. Be a plan.

STRYDER. Oh Nuke, you gone over—you fallen in.

NUKE. No. I thinking with big light on. Think. This place be water, this place be a green world. This place—a place to start again. Build more green worlds. Think. This place have water. This place have green world. No one know. Safe here. Could be a home. Build more green worlds.

STRYDER. No! This is a dump! This no green world! Be too late for greening! This be mine—this plant. Be my green world. Don't make mistake Nuke—this no greening, you speak dreams.

CARSON. We can't let it all disappear . . .

STRYDER. Be quiet fool! Nuke—listen to the street!

NUKE. I stay if that can be.

CARSON. Yes—you can stay.

STRYDER. Fine. Betray the street. Be one with disease. I gone—you be history.

NUKE. History is the taking.

STRYDER. Say what?

NUKE. You heard. Be well Stryder.

CARSON. My plant . . .

NUKE. The plant be her need—let it go . . .

(STRYDER *walks to edge of stage and gets on bike. About to leave when stops.*)

STRYDER. No. Not right. Nuke is right. Carsno. Can't be part of the taking. Must bring back the green world. Bring it back. There still be time. There still be hope. Carson! Nuke! Strange—fighting for a green world from the land of trash. Who would believe . . .

(STRYDER *returns to* NUKE *and* CARSON. NUKE *pushes* STRYDER *to* CARSON. STRYDER *hands plant to* CARSON, *who takes flower and puts it into greenhouse. They stare at the green world in wonder.*)

NUKE. Good head glow Stryder.

CARSON. Yeah—good head glow.

# A Strange Visitor

The outer space intelligence
who hovered over my desk,
a glowing vibrating sphere,
one foot in diameter,
asked me endless questions, for instance:
"What were you doing before I appeared?"
and "Why?" and "For what reason?"
to which I replied I was reading the newspaper
to be informed about what was going on
in the world, and explained the nature
of money and economics and capitalism and communism
and inflation and crises and wars and nations
and borders and territorial expansion and history—
Then he asked me what the other creature
(my two-year-old daughter) was doing.
I said she was playing on the broadloom,
talking to her dolls and herself—
Well, this outer space intelligence rather disappointed me,
for after my succinct answers
he asked such a stupid question
that I suspected he hadn't understood anything at all,
the question being: "How many years does it take
for a wrinkled, wrought-up human baby
like you behind a desk, to shrink into a happy,
light-hearted being like the one on the rug?"

ROBERT ZEND

## ZOO

Edward D. Hoch

The children were always good during the month of August, especially when it began to get near the twenty-third. It was on this day that the great silver spaceship carrying Professor Hugo's Interplanetary Zoo settled down for its annual six-hour visit to the Chicago area.

Before daybreak the crowds would form, long lines of children and adults both, each one clutching his or her dollar, and waiting with wonderment to see what race of strange creatures the Professor had brought this year.

In the past they had sometimes been treated to three-legged creatures from Venus, or tall, thin men from Mars, or even snake-like horrors from somewhere more distant. This year, as the great round ship settled slowly to earth in the huge tri-city parking area just outside of Chicago, they watched with awe as the sides slowly slid up to reveal the familiar barred cages. In them were some wild breed of nightmare—small, horse-like animals that moved with quick, jerking motions and constantly chattered in a high-pitched tongue. The citizens of Earth clustered around as Professor Hugo's crew quickly collected the waiting dollars, and soon the good Professor himself made an appearance, wearing his many-colored rainbow cape and top hat. "Peoples of Earth," he called into his microphone.

The crowd's noise died down and he continued. "Peoples of Earth, this year you see a real treat for your single dollar—the little-known horse-spider people of Kaan—brought to you across a million miles of space at great expense. Gather around, see them, study them, listen to them, tell your friends about them. But hurry! My ship can remain here only six hours!"

And the crowds slowly filed by, at once horrified and fascinated by these strange creatures that looked like horses but ran up the walls of their cages like spiders. "This is certainly worth a dollar," one man remarked, hurrying away. "I'm going home to get the wife."

All day long it went like that, until ten thousand people had filed by the barred cages set into the side of the spaceship. Then, as the six-hour limit ran out, Professor Hugo once more took the microphone in hand. "We must go now, but we will return next year on this date. And if you enjoyed our zoo this year, telephone your friends in other cities about it. We will land in New York tomorrow, and next week on to London, Paris, Rome, Hong Kong, and Tokyo. Then on to other worlds!"

He waved farewell to them, and as the ship rose from the ground, the Earth peoples agreed that this had been the very best Zoo yet. . . .

Some two months and three planets later, the silver ship of Professor Hugo settled at last onto the familiar jagged rocks of Kaan, and the queer horse-spider creatures filed quickly out of their cages. Professor Hugo was there to say a few parting words, and then they scurried away in a hundred different directions, seeking their homes among the rocks.

In one house, the she-creature was happy to see the return of her mate and offspring. She babbled a greeting in the strange tongue and hurried to embrace them. "It was a long time you were gone. Was it good?"

And the he-creature nodded. "The little one enjoyed it especially. We visited eight worlds and saw many things."

The little one ran up the wall of the cave. "On the place called Earth it was the best. The creatures there wear garments over their skins, and they walk on two legs."

"But isn't it dangerous?" asked the she-creature.

"No," her mate answered. "There are bars to protect us from them. We remain right in the ship. Next time you must come with us. It is well worth the nineteen commocs it costs."

And the little one nodded. "It was the very best Zoo ever. . . ."

# About the Authors

**Toni Cade Bambara** was born in 1939 in New York City. She has written two collections of short stories and a novel, and has edited and contributed to other books. Her themes revolve around African-American life and folklore. She spends much of her time teaching college students and working in film.

**Julian Beltrame** emigrated to Canada from Spineda, Italy. He obtained a job as a newspaper editor and reporter for a number of Canadian papers, spending five years as a wartime correspondent for the *Southam News*. His Halifax story comes from this period.

**Ray Bradbury,** born in 1920, writes novels, short stories, children's books, plays, screenplays, and poems. He has written over 400 stories, most of them fantasy and science fiction. He has received many honours and awards for his writing.

**Ernest Buckler** was born and lived in Nova Scotia until his death in 1985. He received numerous awards for his writings, including honorary degrees from three Canadian universities. He is best known for his first novel, *The Mountain and the Valley*, but he also published many short stories and articles.

**David Byrne** has lived in Canada, the United States, and Scotland, where he was born in 1952. When he and two friends formed the Talking Heads in 1975, his career as an avant-garde rock singer began its upward climb, and he eventually released ten albums. He has also produced solo albums, collaborations, musicals, and films.

**Morley Callaghan,** born in Toronto in 1903, began his writing career at 23 when Ernest Hemingway helped him publish some stories in major Paris literary magazines. During World War II he wrote for the Royal Canadian Navy and chaired the Canadian radio program "Citizen's Forum." He eventually published over 20 books and received many awards for his writings.

**Gladys Cardiff,** part Cherokee of the North Carolina Owl family, was born in Browning, Montana, in 1942. She teaches in a poetry program for schools in Washington, where she went to college and now lives with her family.

**Roch Carrier** was born in the Beauce, Quebec, in 1937. Carrier writes short stories, novels, plays, and essays in French, many of which have been translated into English. His short story "The Hockey Sweater" has become a Canadian classic and is the subject of a highly acclaimed animated film.

**Shirley Daniels** is an Ojibwa poet. Her words have appeared in *The First Citizen* and in two anthologies: *I Am an Indian* and *Many Voices*. Daniels has also worked with the National Museum. She lives in Ontario.

**Edward D. Hoch** was born in Rochester, New York, in 1930. He has written more than ten novels and over 700 short stories, many of them mysteries. Fourteen of his stories have been adapted for television.

**(James) Langston Hughes** was born in Joplin, Missouri, in 1902. He became a leading figure in the Harlem Renaissance movement of the 1920s and 1930s. Hughes died in 1967. Hughes often used rhythms of jazz and blues in his poetry, and many of his verses were later set to music.

**Mavis Jones** is a poet from Vancouver, British Columbia. Her poem "Now" appeared in a collection of Canadian poetry titled *Do Whales Jump at Night?* edited by Florence McNeil.

**Jean Little** was born in 1932 in Taiwan. As she is nearly blind, she spent much of her early life in special education schools as both student and teacher. Her first poem was published when she was eighteen. She now writes full-time using a talking computer and has won two Canadian awards for her many books for young readers.

**Norma Fox Mazer** was born in New York City in 1931. In the 1960s, she began writing short stories and novels for young people. She has also collaborated on several books with her husband, Harry Mazer, a writer of young adult fiction.

**Lensey Namioka** was born in Beijing (formerly Peking), China, in 1929. She began her career as a mathematician but has since written several works of fiction based on Chinese and Japanese legends and traditions. She also writes newspaper and magazine articles on travel and humour.

**Quentin Reynolds** (1902–1965) was a foreign news correspondent during World War II, covering North Africa, Sicily, Teheran, Palestine, and battles on the European continent. He also wrote numerous biographies about famous Americans and American institutions.

**Carl Sandburg** (1878–1967) worked for many years as a newspaper writer in Chicago, Illinois. Later he earned his living as a historian, biographer, and poet. Many of his works focus on the changes that have occurred in United States history. He also wrote humorous stories for children.

**William Shakespeare** (1564–1616) was born in Stratford-on-Avon, England. He wrote 37 plays and more than 150 poems. He is considered by many to be the greatest dramatist who ever lived. No other playwright's works have been read or produced as often as those of William Shakespeare.

**Ian Tamblyn** is a composer and musician as well as a playwright. Currently he is writer-in-residence at The Great Canadian Theatre Company in Ottawa. He has released more than ten record albums, including *Magnetic North,* a collection of environmental music inspired by his observations of gray whales, walruses, and sea otters.

**Mitsuye Yamada** was born in Japan in 1923 when her parents were touring the country. She has been a professor of English literature and a coordinator of women's programs at Cypress College in California.

**Robert Zend** (1929–1985) was born in Budapest, Hungary. Before he emigrated to Canada in 1956, he worked as a cartoonist, columnist, freelance writer, and poet. Beginning in 1958, he worked for the CBC in Toronto where he was a writer, editor, director, and producer.

# Credits

Grateful acknowledgment is given to authors, publishers, and agents for permission to reprint the following copyrighted material. Every effort has been made to determine copyright owners. In the case of any omissions, the Publisher will be pleased to make suitable acknowledgments in future editions.

1 "He Was So Little" from HEY WORLD, HERE I AM! by Jean Little. Reprinted by permission of Kids Can Press Ltd., Toronto, Canada.

2 From GORILLA, MY LOVE by Toni Cade Bambara. Copyright © 1970 by Toni Cade Bambara. Reprinted by permission of Random House, Inc.

13 From *Black Women Writers* at Work edited by Claudia Tate. Copyright © 1983 by Claudia Tate. Reprinted by permission of The Continuum Publishing Company.

15 "The Wild Goose" by Ernest Buckler from *Canadian Stories of Action and Adventure.* Used by permission of the Canadian Publishers, McClelland & Stewart, Toronto.

25 "Do You Really Think It's Fair", from SUMMER GIRLS LOVE BOYS AND OTHER STORIES by Norma Fox Mazer. Copyright © 1982 by Norma Fox Mazer. Used by permission of Dell Books, a division of Bantam Doubleday Dell Publishing Group, Inc.

45 "Perhaps the Trees Do Travel" by Roch Carrier. Reprinted with permission of Stoddart Publishing Co. Limited, 34 Lesmill Road, Don Mills, Ontario.

49 Reprinted by permission of Gladys Cardiff.

52 Copyright © 1936, Crowell-Collier Publishing Co. Reprinted by permission of the Estate of Quentin Reynolds.

57 From *All the Years of Her Life* by Morley Callaghan © 1959. Reprinted by permission of Macmillan Canada.

65 From *The Langston Hughes Reader* by Langston Hughes. Reprinted by permission of Harold Ober Associates Incorporated. Copyright © 1958 by Langston Hughes. Copyright renewed 1986 by George Huston Bass.